A GUIDED QUEST INTO THE REALMS
OF TRANSFORMATION

I0518371

REALMS
OF
REFLECTION

Q. T. BOONE

ISBN (Paperback): 979-8-9992648-0-0
ISBN (Hardback): 979-8-9992648-1-7

www.AetherRealRetreats.com

TABLE OF CONTENTS

Acknowledgment

To Chris—my love, my anchor, my home. Thank you for believing in me through every moment of doubt, and for holding space for my growth with patience, laughter, and devotion. Your love lives in these pages.

To Chisom Ezeh—thank you for editing this work with care, clarity, and deep respect for the vision. You helped shape this story into its truest form.

To the beta readers who followed the path after me—thank you for walking with courage and curiosity. Your trust in this journey helped light the way.

And to you, the reader—
May this journey ignite something powerful within you.
May it inspire you to reflect, reclaim, and rise.

This book is dedicated to everyone standing at the intersection of creativity, identity, and resilience. You are the reason this work exists.

INTRODUCTION:
AN INVITATION TO SEEK

I have always been someone who refused to stay comfortable in areas of life that no longer served me. Comfort was never designed for souls like mine or for anyone brave enough to seek a higher purpose.

Now, don't get me wrong—there's nothing wrong with feeling at ease in the life you were born into. Many find peace in the familiar, in the predictable, but that's not me. Ever since I was a child, I longed for something more. My imagination wandered far beyond the edges of reality, craving adventures in worlds both real and imagined.

And yet, time and again, I was reminded of the "real world" where hustle reigns, where pain is currency, and where harming others is sometimes seen as a path to success. People like me—people like *you*—were discouraged from dreaming too big. We were told to settle, to stay in line, to live within the invisible walls of "what is."

For a long time, I listened. I shrank myself to fit a life far smaller than the one I knew was possible.

Nevertheless, this story is not about me.

It's about *You.*

1

Something led you here. Maybe it was the title that caught your eye, or the artwork that sparked your curiosity. Maybe a friend recommended this book, or maybe, just maybe, something deeper pulled you in. A whisper. A feeling. A knowing. Whatever the reason, here you are, swiping or flipping through the pages of this book.

This isn't just a piece of literature. It's a key. An invitation. A mirror.

Pause for a moment. Close your eyes and listen—not just to these words, but to the voice within. The quiet one. The one that guided you here. The same voice that speaks through me now.

Close your eyes now for 20 seconds and breathe

Can you hear it?

It's whispering that there is more.

More to *you*.

More to your life.

More to this world than you've dared to imagine.

Yes, you, the reader. Or perhaps I should call you *the Seeker*.

This is no ordinary book. What you're holding isn't just a guide—it's an epic journey of self-discovery. It wasn't made to simply inform you. It was crafted to transform you.

In this adventure, you'll venture and explore through six core realms. First embarking here in Reflection, then you will discover Energy, Abundance, Love, Mastery, and Summit. Each one is designed to focus on and elevate a different area of your life.

Every chapter, every realm, every encounter is an invitation to step deeper into the heart of your own story. This particular book calls you to Reflect on what matters, on what you've left behind, and on what it means to return to yourself whole.

So ask yourself now, brave Seeker: Are you ready to step beyond comfort, beyond certainty... and into the extraordinary?

If your answer is yes, then breathe deeply. Listen again to that inner voice. And when you're ready—truly ready—keep reading. Let the pages turn. Let the journey begin.

As you travel through this story, I encourage you to keep a journal, like any true explorer would.

If you don't have one, start here. Write in the margins if you can, highlight what moves you, leave footprints on every page. This is your map now.

CHAPTER 1:
THE THRESHOLD

Imagine yourself in the quiet solitude of your private space. It's here, in this moment of calm, away from the noise and distractions of everyday life, that your journey truly begins. Remember, you are never truly alone on this journey. There will be guides. There will be allies. There will be moments when the path before you feels uncertain, yet you will never walk it blindly.

This journey through the REALMS will challenge you. It will test you, and at the same time, it will transform you.

Soon, very soon, you'll notice something—

A Sign.

A Word.

A symbol, an experience that stands out enough to make you pause. And when it appears, you'll know your journey has begun.

Welcome to the Threshold.

There is no turning back.

The Universe Speaks. Are You Listening?

The signs have always been there, quietly waiting to be noticed. They appear subtly, in moments of stillness, in the spaces between your thoughts—moments often overlooked or quickly dismissed.

Perhaps it's a word you keep hearing, spoken by strangers, repeated on the radio, overheard in passing conversations—a word that follows you persistently.

Maybe it's numbers—11:11, 333, 777—appearing on clocks, receipts, license plates, catching your attention precisely when you least expect it.

It could be a bird outside your window, arriving just as you're lost deep in thought; a feather resting softly in your path; or a gentle breeze whispering secrets only your heart understands.

Maybe it's a feeling—an unshakable knowing that you're destined for something greater, something meaningful, something you don't yet have the words to explain.

Whatever it is, something guided you here. Something called you to pause, to listen.

That was your sign.

Journal Prompt I

Today's Date:

Reclaiming Your Why & Noticing the Nudge

1. When you decided to begin this journey, what did you see, hear, or feel in that moment that told you, this is for me? *(Sensory-based access question)*

2. If that whisper within you could speak clearly, what would it say about what you're ready to become now? *(Personifying inner voice to bypass conscious resistance)*

3. Recall a moment you stepped beyond your comfort zone. As you revisit it now, what qualities within you made that possible and where else could you apply them?

(Accessing a resourceful state for future anchoring. This prompt helps you tune into your inner wisdom—the part of you that already knows your next step. By imagining it as a voice, you bypass fear or overthinking and let your deeper truth come forward.)

These questions don't require perfect answers. They are invitations. Let them open doors within you and trust what comes through.

A Sudden Arrival

The air around you suddenly feels charged, heavy with anticipation, like the moments just before a storm. A subtle metallic scent, like ozone after lightning, curls through the room.

Then, a voice. Deep. Resonant. Edged with something electric.

"Finally."

The word reverberates through you, felt more than heard, resonating in your chest like a struck chord.

"You've kept us waiting."

You turn.

Standing before you is a man whose presence instantly draws everything into focus.

His skin, a rich, deep brown, catches the glow of a nearby lantern. Dark waves of hair fall loosely back from his brow, and behind a pair of brass-rimmed goggles, his amber eyes smolder—not with fire, but with something older. Something knowing. He looks at you as if he's been expecting you for quite some time.

His long leather coat is weathered, stitched with metallic inlays—gears, coils, tiny orbs of dim blue light. His belt is lined with tools and oddities, objects whose purpose feels both mysterious and necessary. A faint hum rises from the clasp at his chest, like it's syncing with the pulse in your own body.

He flips a gold coin between his fingers fluidly, without looking. And when he speaks again, it's with the ease of someone who has stood at many thresholds before.

"You felt it, didn't you? A knowing. That quiet shift. That whisper inside. That was no coincidence." He pauses. "It was your initiation."

A flicker of light bursts across the ceiling. Lightning? Imagination? You can't be sure. But what *is* certain is the warmth radiating from him, the steady current of presence he brings.

And then he says, simply: "I'm Eric, the Igniter." He lets the name settle in the space between you before continuing. "I've walked through more doorways than most, but I don't open them for just anyone. I'm here because you're ready—not for *answers*, but for action."

He flips the coin once more, catching it without looking. His smile holds something sly, but sincere. "You could say I'm the first spark on this journey. The one who reminds you of something you forgot—that you have the power to choose your direction, no matter where you've come from."

He tilts his head, eyes steady on yours.

"You want transformation? Then stop waiting for permission. Stop waiting for conditions to be perfect. Stop waiting for fear to go quiet before you move."

He leans in slightly.

"Be the one who begins."

A moment passes.

"Call me a guide, if that helps. But I'm no guru. I'm not here to hand you a map. I'm here to remind you that the compass has always been in your hands." He gestures toward the edges of the room where something—energy, light, possibility—begins to shimmer. "And this?" He grins. "This is just the beginning."

He takes a step back, motioning toward the growing portal with a sweep of his gloved hand.

"There are others you'll meet. Each carries a piece of what you need—reflections of power, insight, courage. But they can only walk beside you. This path?" He nods. "It's yours to claim. And now... we enter."

The Igniter's Introduction

Eric glances around, as though weighing his next words carefully. His eyes settle back on you with that signature glint—the kind that says he's about to do something just a little bit unexpected.

"Alright," he says, his voice dropping an octave as he shifts his weight. The playful energy still dances in his expression, and yet there's a gravity beneath it now. "You're probably comfortable—journal nearby, warm drink in hand—getting ready for a quiet read."

He chuckles, a knowing sound that gently breaks the stillness.

"However..." He pauses, letting the silence stretch like a breath held too long. His fingers tap lightly on the desk. "This journey doesn't happen from the comfort of that chair."

Eric steps back, gaze narrowing as if tuning in to something just beyond the visible. A stillness follows, quiet, heavy, expectant. Then, with a swift motion, he raises his hand toward the far corner of the room. His fingers curl, grasping for something unseen.

You hear it before you see it—a faint hum, a soft vibration in the air. The same energy you felt when you first opened this book. A quiet pulse, steady like a heartbeat.

His eyes stay fixed, focused on the space before him. "Remember," he says gently, "you chose this. Every step from here is yours."

9

With a flick of his wrist, the air ripples, like water breaking under light. A circle of iridescent energy slowly forms before him, glowing at the edges like it's alive. A portal. Breathing. Waiting.

The room shifts. The quiet solitude you once sank into is replaced with a current of charged possibility. The hum grows louder, and strange shadows flicker across the walls.

Eric turns to you again. The grin remains, except that there's something deeper now. A quiet reverence in his voice.

"This," he says, pointing at the portal, "is where the real journey begins. No more books. No more hiding in the margins. Just... you. And what waits on the other side."

He steps forward, eyes locked with yours.

"Are you ready to walk through? To step out of what you know and into what you're becoming?"

A pause lingers.

"Seeker," he continues softly, "you can stay here. Close the book. Walk away. Or... you can step through. From this moment on, the path is yours to shape."

He studies you with quiet understanding. He's not demanding. He's inviting.

Then comes the grin again, lightly awkward, slightly brave.

"Will you let me ignite the flame?" He chuckles. "Yeah... sounded better in my head. A little dramatic. All while true."

His tone settles, steady and clear.

"I'm not here to lead you," he says. "I'm here to light something you already carry. A spark you may have buried under noise, fear, or routine. My role? Just to remind you that it still burns."

His amber eyes soften.

"You're not here by accident. Something in you knows you're ready."

He raises his hand again—this time instead to offer.

"Before you step through, take a moment with yourself. I won't ask for answers... just your honesty."

"Is there a fire you once carried, buried beneath silence and shrouds? What have you been quietly longing for, although afraid to name? Are you stepping into this journey to prove something... or to finally release something?"

He nods gently.

"Let those questions walk with you. Let them burn if they must. Sometimes, it's not the answers that free us—it's daring to ask."

He steps aside.

The portal breathes—soft blues and golden hues swirling like light and breath braided together. It pulses in rhythm, steady and familiar. Like the echo of your own heartbeat.

Time stills. Even the air seems to pause.

Eric's voice carries through the stillness, quiet while still certain.

"Go on," he says. "This is your moment."

You feel it. That subtle shift inside—the part of you that already chose, long before now.

You take a breath. Not just of air but of courage.

And with the quiet fire now stirred within you...

You step into the light.

CHAPTER 2:

STEPPING INTO A NEW WORLD

The moment your foot touches the wooden deck of *Aetherforge*, the ship, everything changes.

The wind here is different, rhythmic and alive. It whispers in patterns you can't quite define, a language of promise and mystery. The air is crisp and cool, carrying a scent that's neither salt nor soil, more like static and starlight, humming softly with potential.

Beneath your feet, the deck is solid and smooth, crafted from polished wood that glows beneath the golden light of a setting sun. Despite this, it appears as no ordinary vessel. The boards don't creak beneath your steps. Instead, there's a subtle vibration, a quiet hum, like the heartbeat of something ancient and alive.

Aetherforge itself is a marvel of impossible beauty. Polished brass gleams against curved steel, and intricate pipes wind gracefully along the railings. Wisps of steam drift from carefully placed vents, hinting at machinery beyond comprehension. And yet, this ship transcends invention. Its sails ripple without wind. Sunlight shimmers across its surfaces like it's being invited to dance.

13

This is a vessel never meant to sail the sea below.

Curiosity draws you to the railing. Your breath catches. Far beneath, the Earth stretches outward in an endless tapestry—snow-capped mountains, sun-washed clouds streaked in pink and amber, and skies rolling softly into twilight. There's no rush. No turbulence. Just stillness in motion. The ship glides effortlessly, as if carried by invisible hands. The horizon spills into infinity.

You are no longer where you once were. You have arrived somewhere entirely new.

Behind you, Eric steps onto the deck, his boots clicking softly against the polished wood. He leans casually against the railing, arms folded, eyes twinkling with mischief.

"You doing alright? Not too queasy, I hope?" he teases, tilting his head. He gestures toward your reflection in a nearby brass panel. "You might want to fix your hair—the static from the portal has given you a full-on lightning look."

You reach up instinctively, smoothing your hair as Eric chuckles.

"Don't worry," he adds, waving a hand. "Happens to everyone." A pause. His eyes flash. "Well... everyone *except me*. Electricity and I, we have an understanding."

He snaps his fingers, and a spark crackles briefly between them. Then, with mock gravity, he says, "People keep telling me to lighten up. You know—Igniter?" He pauses, eyebrow raised, waiting.

Silence.

He sighs dramatically. "Alright, alright. My friends say it's a terrible joke too. Moving on."

Meeting Celeste and Ardyn

Eric steps away from the railing, nodding for you to follow him across the expansive deck of the *Aetherforge*. The ship hums gently beneath your feet, the polished wood warm beneath the golden light of the setting sun.

As you walk, Eric slows, glancing your way with that familiar spark in his eye.

"Tell me something," he says casually. "Have you ever felt like you were moving... yet not truly heading anywhere meaningful?"

He doesn't wait for an answer. Just lets the question hang— quiet, potent.

And something inside you stirs.

Ahead, a tall figure stands near the ship's central mast, completely focused on a celestial map unfurled across a wide metallic table. She doesn't move when you approach—not out of indifference, but rather as if immersed in something far beyond this moment.

"Ah, perfect," Eric murmurs. "Let me introduce you to Celeste."

She turns with effortless grace.

A Soldari Elf, Celeste moves like she belongs to the stars themselves. Her silver hair flows down her back like liquid moonlight, catching the sun's fading warmth. Her robe, deep midnight blue, embroidered with constellations, ripples softly as she moves. And her eyes... they hold you still: silver and endless, like mirrored galaxies. Still. Present. Profound.

"Celeste is our navigator and Astral Scholar," Eric explains with reverence. "Without her, we'd be wandering the cosmos with no real direction—just motion."

Celeste inclines her head with a serene smile. "Welcome," she says, her voice low and calm, like twilight settling over a lake. "This journey is inward. We chart both stars... and soul."

Then—

A sharp rhythm of bare footsteps patters across the deck of the ship. Another figure moves briskly past, not stopping, not slowing. You catch only glimpses: a lean, sinewy frame in well-worn leather armor, a pack slung across his shoulder clinking softly with tools. His dark hair, streaked with earthy hues, fans wildly around his face. His eyes, when they briefly meet yours, are sharp, focused and present, all except lingering. He disappears toward the forge in the ship's lower deck, steam and light casting flickering shadows behind him.

Eric chuckles. "That's Ardyn," he says, fondness in his voice. "A Venasari Elf. He's our quartermaster and master craftsman. Always putting priorities first—always building, fixing, refining. Doesn't say much unless it's essential."

Celeste watches the forge for a beat before turning back to you. "Ardyn may seem driven to the point of distance," she says softly, "although beneath that urgency is unwavering clarity. He grounds us in what must be done *now*, so what's coming *next* can even exist."

Eric nods. "Celeste sees where we're going. Ardyn ensures we're actually *ready* for it. They reflect two kinds of wisdom—vision and discipline."

You look between them: one calm as moonlight, the other gone like a spark into flame. Both in service to a journey far greater than themselves.

Sensing your curiosity, Celeste steps a little closer. "Our peoples, the Soldari and Venasari, once belonged to a shared realm. *Anasterian.* A golden age now fragmented by pride and time. Despite this, we carry its essence forward, each in our own way."

Eric folds his arms, looking toward the horizon. "That's kind of the point of all this, isn't it? With grace for both, we remember where we come from while honoring where we go next."

He turns to you, voice gentler now. Then, with a thoughtful expression, he steps closer and leans lightly against the railing.

"You know," he begins, "most people wander through life reacting to what's in front of them. They wake up, do what's expected, handle what's urgent... and yet they never ask where they're actually *trying* to go." He gestures subtly toward Celeste, still standing near the celestial map. "That's why we have Celeste. She holds the vision. She's the one who sees beyond the horizon—who reminds us we're not just drifting through stars. Every journey needs a direction, even if that destination evolves."

Then he turns his gaze toward the direction Ardyn disappeared. "And Ardyn? He's the anchor. The one who brings it all back to action—asks the hard question: 'What matters *right now*? What needs to happen to make the vision real?' He doesn't speak often, but when he does... it moves mountains."

Eric folds his arms, eyes now back on you. "This ship, this crew—we don't exist just to take you on a joyride through the stars. We're here to help you walk through the *realms of your own life*. Reflection. Energy. Love. Mastery. Legacy. Realms where the world inside you starts shaping the world around you."

He lets that land.

"You'll meet others, each one holding a different piece of the puzzle. Nevertheless these two? Celeste and Ardyn? They form the foundation. Without vision, you drift. Without action, you stall. You'll need both if you want to make any real difference out there..." He nods toward the glowing horizon. "Or in here."

A quiet hum rises from the heart of the ship.

Eric's tone softens, and at the same time, grows more certain.

"So ask yourself—not just here on this ship, but in your life... Do you know where you're going? And are you doing what truly matters to get there?"

Conversations in the Great Mess Hall

Eric leads you from the deck into the heart of the ship, where warmth and rich aromas beckon from beyond a polished doorway. The hum of quiet conversation greets you as you step inside the Great Mess Hall, the ship's central gathering place. Soft light filters through crystalline panels above, casting golden patterns over long wooden tables and curved benches. Herbs, spices, and something subtly sweet drift in the air.

At one table, two figures sit in quiet conversation. Their presence radiates composure and depth, and there's something undeniably distinct about them—something ageless.

Eric smiles. "Come on. I want you to meet Kael and Zara, two of our finest Jinn crew members."

Kael looks up first, his silver eyes kind and perceptive. His fit frame is wrapped in blue and white robes, detailed with embroidery that glimmers like morning dew on crystal leaves. Silver hair flows over his shoulders, framing a gently aged face, centered by a precise black mustache and silver goatee.

"Welcome," he says, his voice deep and peaceful. "Zara and I were just reflecting on our people's path. Some stories seem to find us, no matter how far we travel."

Zara smiles as she turns toward you. Her black and gold robes ripple with movement, runes across the hem catching the light like constellations. Her beauty is serene, timeless, carrying both warmth and strength. When she speaks, her voice feels like it's already known to you.

"As Jinn, our lineage stretches across the cosmos," she says gently. "Our ancestors were travelers of great power and harmony. We carry their memory through the ways we live and guide. We are third-generation guardians, not of dominion, but of balance. Our task isn't to rule; it is to remember what was forgotten... and serve what is becoming." Zara's eyes meet yours. "We don't always journey with weapons or missions. Sometimes, our greatest offering is how we *show up*—to others, and to ourselves."

Eric, ever the guide, folds his arms and glances between the two. "Kael here," he says, "is the master of *Sharpen the Saw.* He's all about renewal—making sure your spirit, body, and mind don't burn out while chasing the goal. Without him, the crew would have fallen apart ten times over."

Kael chuckles softly. "Even purpose requires pause."

Eric gestures to Zara. "And Zara? She *is* the embodiment of *Think Win-Win.* She doesn't just look for peace—she builds it. In a crew this diverse, she's the reason we haven't blown up half the time."

Zara smiles gently. "True success lifts everyone involved. If it costs your well-being or someone else's dignity... it's not a real win."

Eric turns back to you, now a little more serious. "See, a lot of people think a hero's journey is just about fighting through obstacles. Real transformation? That comes from tending to the internal, *and* learning how to create harmony in your relationships. You'll face challenges in the Realms that test both."

He pauses, gaze thoughtful.

"You can't give what you don't renew. And you won't make it far if you're always trying to win *alone.*"

Kael gestures to an open seat. "Sit with us a while," he offers warmly. "There is no rush here. Stillness teaches what speed can't."

Before you can respond, Eric clears his throat, flashing his signature grin. "Tempting, I know—except that we've still got a few corners of the ship to explore. And they'll be here when the time's right."

Zara inclines her head, still smiling. "Another time, when stars align."

Eric leans in, mock-whispering as he leads you out. "Just don't ask them for wishes. Common misconception. I made that mistake once."

Kael's eyes twinkle with patience. "Wisdom and guidance, certainly. Wishes? Rarely a good idea."

As you step away from the golden light and gentle hum of the Mess Hall, the air shifts again—warmer now, tinged with the scent of oil, steam, and metal. A stairway winds downward, drawing you deeper into the *Aetherforge.*

Journal Prompt

Energy, Restoration & Shared Success

1. Where in your life are you most "on" for others and what sensation in your body tells you it's time to replenish?
   (Mind-body awareness and metaphor anchoring)

2. Imagine your energy fully restored. What would you see yourself doing differently and what would others notice in you?
   (Future pacing with behavioral feedback loop)

3. When have you succeeded at the cost of your peace or relationships and what belief was driving that decision?
   (Bringing unconscious motivations to light)

Kael reminds you to return to your roots. Zara reminds you to rise with others. Both are needed to walk this journey well.

The Heart of the Ship – Meeting Finn and Thalia

"This," Eric announces with pride as you arrive before a wide brass door, "is the boiler room—the beating heart of the *Aetherforge*."

He pushes the door open, and a wave of warmth and rhythm washes over you. The room pulses with life—steam pipes hissing softly, gears clicking in harmony, and the steady hum of the ship's engine thrumming beneath your feet like a living heartbeat. Among the maze of valves and glowing mechanisms, two figures are deep in motion. Closest to the great boilers is Thalia—vibrant red hair tied back, streaked with soot and sweat. Their attire is a patchwork of leather, brass, and sturdy fabrics, all marked with grease and purpose. They work quickly, adjusting pressure valves with fluid precision, as if in conversation with the machine itself.

They glance up and grin wide. "Ah, Eric, you've brought company!" Thalia says, wiping their brow with a smudged sleeve. Their voice is bright, warm, and magnetic, full of the kind of energy that makes you feel instantly at ease.

Eric smiles. "Thalia and I go way back—Varne Roe. City of pirates, outlaws, and more rules about who you're supposed to be than stars in the sky."

Thalia laughs, tapping a dial confidently. "Out here," they say, "we get to build things that actually matter. No masks. Just truth and teamwork."

Eric gestures across the room, where another presence has been watching in still silence. "And this," he says, "is Finn, our Jontel warrior and engine guardian."

Finn steps into view. He is massive. His frame radiates quiet strength—shoulders broad, posture unwavering. Dark skin is marked by tattoos and scar-lines that speak of history and discipline. His locs fall over one eye, the other sharp and steady. Around his armor, feathers and carvings evoke something tribal, ancient, and intentional. He offers a respectful nod.

"Well met," he says, his voice low and deep, like thunder on the horizon.

Eric's voice lowers slightly with respect. "Finn's people—the Jontel—are split between warrior queens and warrior kings. Discipline, tradition, and clarity of purpose. He listens more than he speaks. And when he *does* speak..." Eric gestures. "You listen."

Finn's gaze lingers on you for a moment. "There is power in listening," he says simply. "And in restraint."

Thalia chuckles, slinging a wrench onto a magnetic belt. "Meanwhile, I'm more of a 'try-everything-twice-and-learn-as-you-go' type."

Eric laughs. "That's what makes them perfect." He turns to you, voice sincere. "**Thalia embodies synergy**—collaboration, creativity, fast motion with a beating heart behind it. Without them, we wouldn't just stall—we'd *stop*. **Finn embodies deep understanding.** Not just hearing, but also *knowing*. He teaches us to pause, listen, and only then, act."

Thalia grins. "And if anything breaks, we fix it. Together."

Eric gives both crew members a nod of appreciation. "Keep the engines purring. We'll catch up soon."

He leads you up the winding stairs. The air cools as you ascend, the scent of steam giving way to the fresh wind of the upper deck. At the top, the ship stretches before you once more in all its wonder. However Eric doesn't pause for long.

"There's still someone you haven't met," he says, a playful glint returning to his eye. He gestures grandly toward a set of ornate double doors ahead—brass-trimmed and intricately carved with symbols you've yet to learn. They seem to pulse softly, as though expecting you.

"The *Captain*," Eric says, his voice taking on mock solemnity. "Charismatic. Bold. And, if I may say... devastatingly handsome." He winks, and you're not quite sure whether he's serious or joking. "Can't start your journey proper without meeting him," Eric adds, placing a hand on the door. "After all, he's the one guiding this whole thing."

Then, with a grin that holds more mystery than mischief, he pushes the doors open and beckons you inside.

"Come. It's time to meet the man in charge."

CHAPTER 3:

MEETING THE CAPTAIN

You follow Eric through a narrowing corridor that opens beneath an enchanted dome. Overhead, unfamiliar constellations shimmer in deliberate, shifting patterns. The stars pulse with a rhythm that feels just out of reach, as though trying to speak a language you once knew and also forgot.

"The *Aetherforge* doesn't just sail through skies," Eric says quietly beside you. "It sails through possibility—every path, every version of the future that might be."

The hum of the ship beneath your feet seems to echo his words.

He taps his temple. "It moves as our minds do, forward and at the same time outward. The secret is not control. It's trust. Move with purpose... and the right path finds you."

Ahead, double doors gleam under lantern light—dark wood inlaid with golden patterns, their centers marked with brass emblems: flames and lightning intertwined. They glow faintly, pulsing like a heartbeat.

Eric pauses before them and breathes in deeply. "Welcome," he says. "To the heart of it all."

He pushes the doors open. The Captain's Quarters, a space that hums with quiet authority and lived-in purpose. The room is large, and yet not imposing—more workshop than throne room. Maps sprawl across the walls, annotated with countless hand-drawn notes. Books line the shelves in gentle disarray. Tools, charts, and celestial instruments sit arranged with the kind of precision only a restless mind could maintain.

There's a warmth here. A pulse. The kind of place where vision isn't just dreamed but acted on.

Eric strolls in like he belongs here, because he does. He makes his way to a carved desk beneath a wide, curved window. Beyond it, the sky unfolds in an ocean of twilight and drifting clouds.

He leans casually against the desk, offering that familiar, crooked grin.

"So," he begins, "allow me to formally introduce you to our esteemed Captain."

You glance around, instinctively searching for the figure in question.

Eric chuckles, arms folding. "Surprise," he says. "You're looking at him."

You blink. His grin widens. "I know! I'm not exactly the 'captain's uniform and command bark' type."

He gestures around the room with a mix of pride and humility. "Nevertheless I've been preparing this journey longer than you know. The crew, the *Aetherforge*, this route through the Realms, none of it happened by accident." His tone softens slightly, becoming more grounded. "You see, being Captain isn't about waiting for orders. It's about creating the conditions for change. It's about acting with intention, even when the path ahead is unclear. I learned that the hard way, back when I thought life would hand me clarity if I just waited long enough."

He pauses, then smiles gently. "I stopped waiting. I started *choosing*. And this ship? This crew? This journey? All of it came from that choice." He steps forward, his gaze steady now—no longer teasing. "That's why *you're* here. Because something inside you already knows it's time to move. To stop reacting. To begin becoming."

Eric turns to the wide window, letting the silence linger a moment.

"Now that you've met the crew, the ship, and me... it's time to understand what this is really about. Where we're going and why you're the one who needs to go there."

You continue to look around the room. A brass table surrounded by worn leather chairs speaks of strategy, stories, and memory. At the far end, a wide window curves outward into the twilight sky—a view that stretches into forever. However, your eyes are drawn elsewhere. Near the edge of the desk, beneath the soft glow of an oil lamp, sits a simple silver locket. Its chain loops loosely around the lamp's base. The metal is worn, the surface weathered by time. You move toward it instinctively.

Eric watches you, and for a moment, the ever-present glint in his eye dims—not lost, only gentled.

"Ah," he murmurs. "You found it."

You pick it up. It's heavier than expected—quiet with meaning.

"That belonged to my grandmother," Eric says softly. "She was the first to believe in me—*really* believe. Gave it to me the day I was supposed to graduate from the Academy."

He approaches the desk, resting his hand against it like it holds him upright.

"She told me, 'This is for the captain you will become.' I didn't understand. Not then." His voice catches for a moment, his eyes focused—not on you, but on the memory. "I wasted that chance. Coasted through my final year. Thought talent would carry me. Showed up late. Laughed off the work. Led my first skirmish with arrogance... and nearly lost my crew."

The words fall heavily between you, and in them, something raw lingers.

"She still believed in me. Told me I could turn it around. That I still had time."

Eric's gaze lingers on the locket in your hand. He smiles faintly. The warmth doesn't quite reach his eyes.

"She didn't give it to me. Not then. And I don't blame her. I hadn't earned it."

Silence stretches—thick with what he isn't saying.

"I repeated my final year. Faced every hard thing I'd run from. Led a second skirmish with everything I had and earned my title the right way."

He lifts his eyes, voice steady, though softer now.

"When I returned to Varne Roe, ready to show her who I'd become... she was gone." Eric's voice falters. "She passed before I could share that moment with her. Before I could prove I'd become the man she always saw in me."

He reaches gently for the locket, holding it now with both hands. The weight of it seems different physically while at the same time representing something ancestral and emotional.

"She never gave it to me herself. But after she was gone, I found it in her chest, wrapped in the same cloth she used to keep her healing herbs."

He pauses, thumb brushing the metal.

"She knew. Even then. She believed in me even after I stopped believing in myself."

A long silence follows.

Then, as if released from some unseen pressure, a tear slips down Eric's cheek. He doesn't wipe it away. He just lets it fall.

"She's the reason I stopped waiting. Stopped hoping someone else would choose for me. I didn't need more time. I needed to *begin*."

He exhales slowly, and when he looks up, his voice is quieter and yet steadier.

"And that... is when I met my Moyux."

The word lands like a stone in still water.

He sets the locket down with care, letting his fingers rest on it for a breath before pulling away.

"A Moyux," he says, meeting your gaze, "isn't just a monster. It's the *Manifestation of Your Unintegrated eXperiences.* The guilt you bury. The hesitation you justify. The patterns you know are holding you back, and yet you keep feeding."

He lets the words settle before continuing.

"For me, it was fear disguised as pride. Inaction dressed up as independence. The voice that told me, 'Don't try, you'll only fail again.' That was my Moyux."

He walks slowly to the center of the room, turning toward the curved window. Twilight stretches endlessly beyond the glass.

"We all have one. Sometimes more than one. And they don't always look like monsters. Sometimes they show up as silence. Or perfectionism. Or trying to please everyone except yourself." He turns back to you. "The Moyux takes on the shape of whatever we haven't yet faced. It feeds on avoidance, shame, and survival strategies that no longer serve us."

His expression softens, free of performance now, just presence. "Nevertheless the only way forward is through. You don't outrun the Moyux. You meet it. You understand it. And when you do... you reclaim the part of yourself it's been holding hostage."

Eric moves beside you again, voice lowered to a whisper meant just for you.

"So let me ask you, Seeker..."

He tilts his head slightly, eyes steady.

"Have *you* ever hesitated when it mattered most? Ever felt the pull to act and let it pass?"

A beat. No pressure. Just an invitation.

"Have you ever had someone believe in you so deeply that you couldn't see it yourself? Someone who *knew* what you could become, even before you did?"

He lets the silence speak for a moment.

"If so… then you're not alone." He gestures gently toward the glowing stairwell, spiraling downward into soft light. "The journey begins below and yet what matters more is what you're willing to carry with you." He smiles with calm resolve. "We don't need you to be perfect. We just need you to be *honest.* That's how it starts."

Journal Prompt

As Eric's words settle deeply within you, the gentle hum of the *Aetherforge* seems to echo his wisdom, inviting you into a space of honest introspection. Understanding Eric's story has illuminated the presence of your own Moyux—the fears, hesitations, and doubts that may have quietly influenced your path.

Write openly, allowing yourself vulnerability and clarity. In facing your Moyux (**Manifestation of Your Unintegrated eXperiences)** through this reflective practice, you take an essential step toward personal growth, empowerment, and genuine self-awareness.

1. What specific voice or image comes up when self-doubt shows up and what's the first shift that weakens its grip?
   (Sensory submodality shift – useful for deconstructing fear)

2. If that avoided truth could be seen as a guide instead of a threat, what wisdom would it be trying to offer you?
   (Reframing resistance as inner guidance)

3. Close your eyes and imagine stepping forward as if you already felt courageous. What shifts in your breath, posture, or intention?
   (Somatic anchoring into a desired state)

You don't have to conquer your Moyux all at once. Facing it is the true path to transformation.

Celeste's Timely Interruption

A gentle, soothing voice from the doorway breaks the profound silence of the room, softly drawing you and Eric back into the present.

"Reflection is indeed powerful, Eric," the intruder says gently, their words filled with quiet warmth, "but there's also strength in knowing when it's time to move forward."

You turn, finding Celeste standing calmly at the entrance, her presence a reassuring balm, gracefully shifting the mood from heavy introspection toward hopeful anticipation. Eric offers her a soft, grateful smile, visibly relaxing under her calming influence.

"You always have a way of arriving exactly when you're needed most," Eric says warmly, his voice regaining its steady confidence.

Celeste moves gracefully into the room, her steps almost silent against the polished wooden floor. Her eyes hold a deep understanding, reflecting empathy and gentle encouragement as she acknowledges Eric's vulnerability.

"Timing is a delicate balance," she replies softly with a reassuring warmth. "And balance, as you well know, is my specialty."

Eric chuckles gently, visibly lighter now, the tension of his past easing into a quiet sense of acceptance.

Celeste turns toward you, her expression kind and inviting. "If you're ready," she says calmly, "I think it's time we reveal the path ahead."

Eric nods, encouraging you silently with a knowing smile.

You rise slowly, sensing that Celeste's guidance will gently lead you forward from reflection into purposeful action. Together, you prepare to journey deeper into the mysteries awaiting you.

Welcoming into the Map Chamber

Celeste gently guides you through the softly illuminated corridors of the *Aetherforge*, each step forward feeling purposeful and reassuring. The atmosphere subtly shifts from intimate reflection to a sense of quiet excitement and anticipation. Eric walks beside you, his presence strong yet comforting, a steady reassurance as you move toward whatever lies ahead.

At last, you arrive at an ornate doorway, its surface etched with graceful patterns that pulse faintly with a serene, celestial blue glow. Celeste pauses, turning toward you with a calm, inviting expression.

"Welcome to the Map Chamber," she announces softly, her voice echoing gently with reverence.

The doors glide open silently, revealing an awe-inspiring room. Circular in shape, the chamber's walls radiate with gentle, shimmering light, intricate carvings forming constellations and celestial paths that seem alive, shifting softly with ethereal grace.

At the chamber's heart, you notice Celeste's physical form seated calmly, cross-legged in a lotus position, eyes closed in serene meditation. Momentarily, you're puzzled, glancing from the figure beside you to the one seated quietly.

"Astral projection," Celeste explains gently, noticing your curiosity. "My consciousness travels freely, guiding us through the paths of possibility, while my physical form maintains harmony here."

With practiced ease, Celeste's astral form steps forward, merging effortlessly with her seated body. Her eyes slowly open, shimmering gently as she rises to her feet with fluid grace, fully present and focused.

"This chamber is where we chart our course through the Realms of Transformation," she explains warmly, gesturing toward the celestial patterns glowing around you. "Together, we'll navigate the path ahead, uncovering truths, facing challenges, and embracing the wisdom waiting within."

Eric nods thoughtfully, stepping aside slightly, signaling the space is now fully yours, ready for exploration. Celeste smiles gently, offering her hand, her gesture warm yet weighted with anticipation.

"Come," she says softly, her voice almost reverent, "it's time to step into your story."

As you take her hand, the doors to the Map Chamber close quietly behind you, enveloping you in an expectant silence. The air grows charged, each breath carrying the gentle promise of discovery. Celeste leads you forward, her steps graceful, purposeful, guiding you gently toward the heart of the room where the celestial map waits, softly glowing.

With each step, the lanterns overhead pulse gently, mirroring the quickening rhythm of your heartbeat, as though the ship itself senses the significance of what's about to unfold.

Celeste pauses briefly, glancing toward the star map as its constellations flicker into vivid, purposeful clarity. Then she turns, her eyes luminous in the dim light.

"Together," she whispers encouragingly, "let's enter the Realm of Reflection."

CHAPTER 4:

ARRIVAL INTO MYTHOS

The air within the *Aetherforge* grows noticeably still as the ship gently drifts into the Realm of Reflection. Within the Map Chamber, the atmosphere shifts subtly, carrying an unmistakable sense of entering sacred space. Through wide, gracefully curved windows, an ethereal glow of deep indigo cascades gently inward, painting the polished wooden panels and brass fixtures in hues of starlight and shadow. The gentle hum of the ship softens to a whisper, as though even the *Aetherforge* itself holds its breath in reverent anticipation.

The crew gathers around the central platform of the Map Chamber, their eyes instinctively drawn upward. Above, the chamber's majestic dome comes alive. A vast and mesmerizing celestial projection stretches across the curved ceiling, vividly recreating the boundless indigo sky of the realm outside. Countless silver points of starlight shimmer gently, suspended as though woven from threads of living light, each pulse matching your heartbeat, a subtle dance inviting contemplation and curiosity.

Celeste steps gracefully to the forefront, her movements deliberate yet serene. Extending one hand upward, she carefully traces invisible threads through the projected heavens, guiding the magical illumination with practiced precision. In response, the projected stars awaken, shifting positions as though recognizing the touch of an old friend. The celestial patterns gradually form, coalescing into a luminous, ethereal vision within the heart of the chamber.

Slowly, deliberately, threads of starlight twist and spiral gracefully together, converging into the radiant figure of a woman suspended gently in midair. Her presence is powerful yet deeply calming, radiating wisdom and profound melancholy. The crew murmurs softly, their voices respectfully hushed, careful not to disturb the magical vision now clearly defined before them.

"The Seer," Celeste breathes reverently, her voice filled with awe and deep respect. "Mother of all Elves. Guardian of truths."

The Seer's image floats serenely above the crew, her hands delicately extended before her. In them, she holds an object shimmering with pure, brilliant silver light, a mirror unlike any other. Its reflective surface shifts subtly, glowing softly, beckoning gently as if aware of your presence. It's more than glass and silver; it feels like a doorway, a passage into unseen depths, holding countless truths waiting patiently to be known.

Celeste lowers her hand slowly, her silver eyes glinting with profound seriousness as she turns gently toward you. Her gaze holds steady, full of compassion and quiet strength.

"This is the crossroads of transformation," she says, her voice barely above a whisper. "The Realm of Reflection calls to each of us, offering an extraordinary gift to those who are courageous enough to confront what lies within."

The crew stands quietly, respectfully, granting space to the gravity of this moment. Eric crosses his arms thoughtfully, his expression serious yet reassuringly calm. Celeste stands near him, her gaze gently reverent, deeply attuned to the vision she's summoned. Ardyn shifts subtly beside them, his sharp eyes alert and watchful, quietly assessing the unfolding scene.

Finn remains solemn and still, his powerful frame grounding him securely, fingers wrapped steadily around the handle of his massive axe—a silent guardian ready to face whatever may arise. Kael and Zara stand slightly apart, their posture elegant yet deeply attentive, observing intently with expressions of thoughtful serenity. Thalia stands near Finn, hands lightly clasped, their eyes bright with curiosity yet tempered by quiet respect, absorbing every detail with unwavering focus.

The ship continues drifting gently, held safely within the quiet embrace of the Realm. All around is stillness, a silent pause awaiting your next move. Above, the Seer's silver form gazes softly downward, mirror in hand, patient as eternity itself. Her presence is both comforting and daunting—an ancient wisdom beckoning softly from within the reflective depths of the mirror she guards.

You step forward, feeling the soft, rhythmic pulse of starlight on your skin. Something shifts inside, an awareness unfolding gently, a recognition that whatever comes next will mark a turning point.

The Seer Constellation

As you stand beneath the gentle gaze of the Seer's shimmering image at the center console of the Map Chamber, Celeste steps forward once more, her voice clear and melodic, carrying a timeless weight. Her eyes remain fixed reverently upon the celestial figure, shimmering with reflected starlight.

"Long before our journey began, long before the *Aetherforge* first sailed these skies," she begins softly, "there stood a city of wonders named Anasterian. It was an era of peace, understanding, and profound unity, inhabited by two proud Elven lineages— the Venasari, wild and attuned with nature, and the Soldari, wise and deeply connected to the stars. At the heart of their shared harmony lived their revered matriarch, the Seer."

The starlight around the Seer begins to shift gently, illustrating Celeste's story, painting vivid images of a magnificent city. Towers rise gracefully, glittering crystalline structures bathed in gentle starlight. Streets weave through vibrant gardens filled with luminous plants and flowing waters that shine like liquid silver. It's a vision of tranquility, balance, and beauty.

"The Seer was gifted with profound foresight," Celeste continues, her voice thick with admiration and quiet sadness. "She could clearly glimpse countless futures, each possibility unfolding before her eyes like threads woven into a vast tapestry of fate."

The celestial imagery above darkens gently, illustrating her words vividly, stars shifting into a haunting scene: division and conflict emerging among the elves. The once unified city of Anasterian fractures, becoming distant fragments adrift across the expanse of the Aetherlands. Expressions of sorrow appear on the faces of those watching the vision unfold.

"Yet her gift of vision became her greatest sorrow," Celeste explains, her voice subdued. "She foresaw her beloved people turning away from each other, lost in pride, fear, and misunderstanding. She warned them, pleaded with them to turn inward, to seek truth and harmony within themselves first. But they chose blame over reflection, discord over understanding, fulfilling her tragic prophecy."

The celestial image gently shifts back to the Seer, now alone and deeply sorrowful, retreating quietly into isolation. The silver mirror she holds gently takes shape, its reflective surface shining brilliantly even in her solitude.

"Heartbroken, but never defeated, the Seer retreated into solitude, crafting her final legacy—the Mirror of Sovereignty," Celeste explains, her voice growing warmer, hopeful. "A mirror of reflection, but also a tool of transformation. Within it, she poured her wisdom, hope, and unyielding belief that true harmony and clarity can only be discovered through courageous self-reflection."

The celestial figure now gazes gently downward toward the crew, her silver mirror held forward, inviting each observer into its reflective embrace.

Celeste turns once more, her eyes meeting yours with quiet resolve. "The Seer's lesson remains clear: before we can find peace or connection with others, we must first face the truths hidden within ourselves," she says softly with conviction. "Are you prepared to embrace the lesson she left behind, to step boldly into the power of your reflection?"

Mirror of Sovereignty

As the celestial image of the Seer softly fades, Celeste extends her hand toward the mirror still shimmering gently in the starlight, its reflective surface luminous and inviting. The crew stands respectfully silent, their eyes fixed upon this object of profound significance, sensing the gravity of the moment.

"The Mirror of Sovereignty," Celeste begins, her voice filled with reverence and quiet wonder. "This relic is far more than mere glass or silver. It holds within it the clarity and truth of the Seer herself, carefully crafted as her final gift to those willing to seek understanding and wisdom."

The mirror's surface seems to ripple subtly, as though stirred by an invisible hand, revealing brief flashes of images, moments from countless lives woven gently into its reflective depths. Celeste continues her explanation, her tone gentle and clear, offering both understanding and guidance.

"It reflects not what you show the world, but what you hold hidden deep within yourself. It unveils your true fears, your deepest desires, your genuine self beyond the illusions or expectations that others place upon you. To gaze into it is an act of courage, for it asks you to confront all that you are and all you have been afraid to become."

Her silver gaze meets yours again, holding steady with compassion and certainty.

"The Mirror of Sovereignty offers the powerful gift of true self-awareness and inner sovereignty. It encourages you to reclaim your power and authenticity, to see clearly past the doubts, fears, and falsehoods you've allowed to limit your journey. Within its depths, you will discover the clarity necessary to navigate your life with purpose, confidence, and true inner harmony."

Celeste pauses, allowing her words to settle deeply. She lowers her hand slowly, the mirror's reflection settling back into quiet stillness, awaiting the next brave soul willing to approach.

"Remember," she concludes gently, "to confront your reflection is to truly know yourself without the need to judge. And in knowing yourself fully, you begin to heal, grow, and embrace the path toward the life you've always imagined."

The crew stands in silent agreement, each deeply reflective, clearly acknowledging the weight and promise of the Mirror's lesson. The mirror calls softly to you, its reflective surface patient, gentle, and endlessly wise. The *Aetherforge* seems to breathe softly beneath your feet, awaiting your response, sensing that your decision now will define everything that follows.

Clearly Defined Objectives & Personal Application

As the gentle glow of the celestial mirror fades softly back into the tapestry of stars, Celeste turns to face you fully, her expression serene yet intent, clearly signifying that the symbolic vision has now become a personal invitation. Her voice resonates with a gentle authority, carrying both encouragement and clarity. "Every star, every constellation, every vision we've shared tonight," she begins gently, "holds a deeper purpose. You are not merely an observer here; you're a seeker on a transformative journey. The Realm of Reflection calls directly to you, offering clarity and insight you can carry forward into every aspect of your life."

She steps closer, placing a reassuring hand gently upon your shoulder, her touch warm and steady. "The Mirror of Sovereignty symbolizes your personal power, your authentic self waiting to be recognized and embraced fully. It calls upon you to confront and understand the truths within—to shed illusions, release doubts, and embrace the strength and authenticity that comes from true self-awareness."

She pauses briefly, allowing the profound weight of her words to settle, then continues clearly and warmly.

"As we journey forward, your objective within this Realm is clear: identify the hidden fears, limiting beliefs, or truths you've been avoiding. Embrace them courageously, for in doing so, you reclaim your sovereignty, clarity, and true potential. Reflect deeply, and consider how this understanding will transform your relationships, choices, and path forward."

The crew nods gently in agreement, clearly unified in their purpose and supportive of your personal journey ahead.

Celeste smiles gently, her silver eyes encouraging and unwavering. "Now, take a moment to reflect deeply and honestly within your journal," she advises softly.

Journal Prompt

"Let these questions guide you toward personal clarity and empowerment:"

1. When you hear your inner critic, whose voice does it sound like and what would change if you rewrote that voice in your own tone of love?
   (Voice identification + submodality shift)

2. Picture a moment you felt confident or creative. What strengths were alive in you then and how can you bring them into a current challenge?
   (Resource anchoring with time bridging)

The stars seem to pulse gently in rhythm with your heartbeat, patiently awaiting your response, knowing that your courage to reflect now will illuminate your path clearly and profoundly forward.

CHAPTER 5:
IDENTIFYING THE MOYUX

"Reflection is necessary, while action is essential," Ardyn's voice cuts through the silence, crisp and commanding.

You glance up from your journaling, startled. Standing confidently atop the table you're seated at, Ardyn meets your gaze directly, unfazed by the unusual vantage point his short stature demands. His sharp eyes pierce through any lingering hesitation, his stance firm and authoritative despite—or perhaps because of—his height.

"Celeste's way is gentle and necessary," he acknowledges briskly, hopping lightly down from the table, landing effortlessly. "However, reflection alone won't confront your Moyux. We must face these monsters head-on."

He turns sharply, addressing the gathered crew with swift decisiveness. "Everyone, back to your stations. The Seeker and I have crucial work to do."

Eric, leaning against the wall with crossed arms, gives a reluctant nod. "As you say, Ardyn."

Despite Eric's rank as captain, it's clear Ardyn's assertiveness grants him a unique authority, making him the ideal first mate.

Ardyn gestures briskly, motioning you to follow. "Come along. The Forge awaits. It's time to clearly identify your Moyux and begin preparing for what lies ahead."

You follow Ardyn down a narrow stairway that twists and descends deep into the ship's belly. With each step, the air grows warmer, heavier with the scent of heated metal, oil, and something almost alchemical—an aroma that sharpens your senses and focuses your thoughts.

Entering the Forge, you find yourself surrounded by walls lined meticulously with tools, each placed with exacting precision. Large anvils, polished by countless strikes, stand resolutely throughout the room, reflecting the flickering glow of flames that dance within a massive hearth. It is a place of purpose, of transformation—raw elements reshaped into something more powerful, more meaningful.

Ardyn moves confidently, retrieving tools and arranging his workspace as though following an unseen yet vital blueprint. His efficiency is mesmerizing, each action deliberate and precisely measured.

"Priorities first," Ardyn begins without preamble, eyes not leaving his task. "We face the Moyux head-on, because nothing matters until you clearly understand what stands in your way."

He pauses, turning sharply toward you, eyes keen and uncompromising. "The Moyux isn't just some imaginary beast lurking in your mind. It's the fundamental truth you've ignored, the one you're afraid to name. It's the silent saboteur undermining your every step forward."

Ardyn picks up a small, delicate hammer, turning it thoughtfully in his calloused hands, his voice growing quiet, firm, and resolute.

"You cannot fight what you don't recognize. You can't forge strength without clarity. Identifying your Moyux is the first strike of the hammer—focused, intentional, and essential. Every successful journey begins here, in absolute honesty."

Ardyn carefully sets down the hammer, turning toward you with an intensity tempered by quiet understanding. His eyes narrow slightly, thoughtful yet firm.

"Earlier," he continues, folding his arms and standing squarely before you, "you answered a question: *'What truths about myself have I been reluctant to face, and what am I afraid of discovering?'*"

His tone isn't judgmental, nevertheless there's an unflinching directness that demands honesty—not with him, but with yourself.

"I don't know your answer, Seeker," he continues steadily, his voice softer yet still unyielding. "And frankly, I don't need to. But you do."

He takes a slow step closer, his gaze intense yet gentle, as though he's staring directly at the core of your being. "Whatever truth emerged, whatever you wrote, or perhaps couldn't quite bring yourself to write, that is your Moyux. Facing it isn't easy; it never is. From this point forward, clarity demands courage, and your path begins here."

He pauses, allowing his words to settle, letting you absorb their weight.

"Reflection without action is useless," Ardyn adds firmly, holding your gaze. "You've named your fear. Now, you must understand it deeply enough to overcome it."

Ardyn studies you quietly, his stern gaze tempered by genuine understanding. He steps aside, leading you toward a small table, illuminated gently by the warm, flickering glow of the Forge.

"Now that you've clearly recognized your Moyux," Ardyn says firmly yet compassionately, laying a fresh sheet of parchment and ink-dipped quill deliberately before you, "you must understand its full impact."

He pauses thoughtfully, leaning forward slightly as his voice lowers, becoming deeply earnest.

"How has avoiding these deeper truths shaped your life and the decisions you've made along the way? Reflect carefully," he adds, "because your answer won't just reveal patterns of your past; it will determine the nature of the weapon you'll need for the battles ahead."

Ardyn straightens, stepping back respectfully, granting you space. The gentle, rhythmic hum of the Forge steadies your thoughts, offering reassurance as you prepare to reflect once more, knowing clearly now that understanding your Moyux is the crucial first step toward crafting the strength you'll soon require. He waits quietly, granting you time to complete your reflection. Once finished, he steps forward again, gently yet decisively drawing your attention.

"Good," he acknowledges firmly. "Understanding how your Moyux has influenced your path is vital because reflection alone won't grant you victory."

He moves closer, eyes sharp yet empathetic, and presents one final parchment, positioning it deliberately before you. "You've already considered this," Ardyn states, tapping the parchment meaningfully. "But now, it's time to truly embrace it."

His voice becomes more profound, carrying a strength that feels grounding and empowering. "If you fully embraced these hidden truths, what positive shifts could you create in your life and your future?"

He pauses, allowing the weight of the question to resonate fully before continuing with conviction: "The weakness you identified, your Moyux, is not a burden; it's the foundation upon which you'll forge your greatest strength. Your answer now becomes your blueprint, the raw material from which we'll craft your mission. A statement of purpose so strong, so clear, that your Moyux cannot stand against it."

He straightens, his posture certain and reassuring, his gaze unwavering. "Are you ready to turn your vulnerability into your power?"

Journal Prompt I

Ardyn steps back thoughtfully, giving you the space you need. He gestures toward the parchment, his eyes steady, voice clear yet gentle with understanding. "This moment," he states firmly, "is about honesty. You've glimpsed your Moyux; you've felt its presence, and perhaps you've named it. Now is the time for absolute clarity."

He pauses, his intensity softened by compassion. "Consider deeply, and write the answers clearly and courageously:"

1. If your Moyux had a voice, what would it say to keep you small and what does that voice fear would happen if you grew beyond it?
   (Purpose: Externalizes the limiting belief, accesses the "positive intent" of the inner saboteur, and makes it easier to separate from the self.)
   Example:

   » "Don't speak up, you'll be rejected."

   » "If you fail, no one will love you."

2. Imagine standing face-to-face with your Moyux. What is the exact opposite energy it cannot stand to be in the presence of and when have you felt that power before?
   (Purpose: This accesses the Seeker's core strength by creating a polarity—NLP often works by contrast. They find the antidote in lived memory.)
   Example:

» If the Moyux is fear of rejection → the opposite might be **belonging, boldness, connection**.

» If it's silence → the opposite might be **expression, singing, truth-telling**.

Ardyn stands quietly by, respectfully allowing your thoughts to settle. The Forge around you seems to hum softly, encouraging you to face this reflection bravely, knowing that honesty now will strengthen and empower you for the path ahead.

Ardyn's Story— From Embers to Flame

Ardyn waits quietly as you finish your reflection. His gaze is thoughtful, distant for a moment, as though something in your process has awakened memories long tucked away within himself. The silence lingers, filled only by the gentle, rhythmic pulse of the Forge. At last, he exhales slowly, breaking the quiet.

"You know," he begins softly, his eyes still drawn toward the steady dance of flames in the Forge, "it wasn't always like this for me. Order, clarity, strength—these weren't gifts I was given freely. I had to earn them, fight for them, forge them from chaos itself."

He offers a faint, bittersweet smile, his voice gently shadowed by echoes of past hurts. "Among my people, the Venasari, we honor nature fully. Whispering winds, nurturing waters, lush forests, guiding stars... My kin find beauty in harmony, tranquility, and grace. These are seen as safe, acceptable elements; they reflect what is familiar and comfortable."

His voice drops slightly, weighted with old memories and quiet pain. "Except that fire was viewed as wild, uncontrollable, even dangerous. It represented chaos, destruction, a force that could burn away everything we valued."

Ardyn shifts slightly, his usually firm posture softened by vulnerability. He seems smaller for a moment, more exposed. "Yet, despite that, I felt a deep, undeniable connection to fire. Perhaps it chose me more than I chose it. To me, it wasn't chaos—it was clarity. It wasn't destruction—it was the potential for creation, reshaping, rebirth."

He hesitates, eyes briefly closing as he summons a difficult memory, his voice tightening with emotion. "And yet choosing fire isolated me. To my kin, I became an outsider. I was already small, easily overlooked, clumsy compared to those naturally gifted. Loving fire only made things worse. They called me reckless, disruptive, unworthy, even dangerous. And because of my own doubts and insecurities, I believed them."

Ardyn meets your gaze, sincerity mingled with quiet strength. "I internalized their judgments—their invisible scripts—those limiting beliefs placed upon me without realizing it. Their fears and prejudices became my truths, hidden deeply in my subconscious. Over time, they shaped my reality: I withdrew, avoided responsibility, became scattered and disorganized. Opportunities passed by because I felt undeserving of them. I convinced myself my passion was a flaw, my height a disadvantage, and my voice not worth being heard."

He pauses meaningfully, giving you space to absorb the weight of his words.

"I almost allowed these invisible scripts to define my entire life," he concludes softly, clearly, "because I didn't recognize them for what they truly were—beliefs forced upon me, not truths I had chosen."

Ardyn's gaze deepens as he recalls something powerful, something transformative. His expression shifts subtly, becoming warm and filled with reverent gratitude.

"Have you ever felt that way, Seeker?" he asks quietly, his voice gentle yet deeply resonant. "Caught in those invisible scripts—limiting beliefs you've internalized from others? Perhaps you've convinced yourself you're not enough, too different, too small, too uncertain to step into your true potential?"

He allows the question to linger briefly, giving you a moment to silently acknowledge your own experiences. Then he takes a slow, steady breath, standing taller, his eyes reignited clearly with determination and strength.

"For me, everything changed the day someone finally saw my difference not as a weakness but as a potential instead. My mentor," he says quietly, voice tinged with deep respect, "was a Venasari Lightbringer named Elyran. A gifted flame keeper—one of the few among my kin who dared harness the power of fire through a profound understanding instead of force."

Ardyn pauses, clearly moved by the memory. "Elyran had once been considered among the greatest of our kind until his path changed dramatically the day he lost control of a powerful fire elemental. The blaze overwhelmed him, burning away his sight and forever scarring his face."

His voice softens even more, gentle admiration evident beneath his words. "Despite losing his vision, despite becoming an outcast, mocked and abandoned by many who once praised him, Elyran never lost his passion, nor did he grow bitter. Instead, his blindness taught him to perceive fire differently. He learned to understand its nature, its rhythms, its whispers rather than attempting to dominate it."

Ardyn's expression deepens thoughtfully. "Elyran taught me that fire is never meant to be controlled through sheer force. To master fire, you must listen first, understand second, and finally, guide it with clarity of intention. 'Respect its strength while honoring your own,' he'd often say."

His voice carries renewed energy now, layered with pride and gratitude. "Elyran's example was my turning point. He showed me that even our greatest failures, our deepest losses, can forge us into something far greater, if we allow them."

He straightens fully now, his posture reflecting newfound pride and unshakable purpose. "In that single moment, I realized I was never wrong or broken. I simply lacked clarity. With this new awareness, I embraced discipline and became deliberate, intentional, focused. My love of fire became my greatest strength. It forged me as surely as I forged metal."

He pauses thoughtfully, letting the significance of his words settle around you before continuing, his voice filled with unwavering conviction: "Seeker, your Moyux is like a powerful fire elemental—raw and untamed. It can burn through you or burn through what it deems irrelevant. When you face it, I promise it will not destroy you…instead it will forge you into something unrecognizable." Ardyn smiles softly, encouragingly. "Believe me, there's no greater feeling than wielding your soul's fire with purpose."

Forging Your Mission— Turning Weakness into Strength

Ardyn nods slowly, recognizing clearly that the moment for action has arrived. His demeanor shifts, becoming purposeful and deliberate, echoing the strength of the Forge surrounding you.

"Your Moyux feeds on doubt, fear, and uncertainty," he says firmly, his voice clear and commanding. "To confront it, you must transform your invisible scripts—those limiting beliefs you've carried—into statements of clarity, courage, and power."

He steps toward the anvil, resting his palm against the sturdy metal surface. "Just as iron is reshaped by fire and strength, your truths can be reshaped by intention and clarity. Your weapon against your Moyux will be your Mission Statement—a powerful declaration of purpose that will guide you forward."

Ardyn gestures to the parchment before you, his voice unwavering: "Start by clearly rewriting your limiting beliefs into empowering truths. For example, if your invisible script says, *'I'm not good enough to succeed,'* reshape it clearly and boldly as: *'I am capable, worthy, and deserving of success, and I will embrace opportunities that come my way.'*"

He pauses, eyes firm yet supportive. "Your mission statement should clearly capture your commitment to action, courage, and growth. It's your battle cry, your guiding principle, a weapon that your Moyux cannot withstand."

Ardyn offers a reassuring nod, clearly sensing that you're ready to move forward. He gestures quietly for you to follow him deeper into the heart of the Forge. "Come," he says gently yet firmly, "it's time to forge your weapon."

He leads you toward the back of the room, to a forge unlike any other you've seen. Its structure is intricate yet ancient, carved from a dark, polished stone etched with delicate runes that shimmer faintly in the firelight. At its center, a flame dances gently—vibrant, alive, and radiating an energy that feels both comforting and deeply powerful.

Ardyn pauses thoughtfully, voice softening in reverence. "This Forge is special. It doesn't merely shape metal. It reshapes intention, beliefs, and truths. Its flame symbolizes renewal. It takes what is tarnished, old, or burdened by invisible scripts and returns it refined, purified, and empowered."

He reaches into his pocket, pulling forth a small, dull, tarnished piece of metal. "This symbolizes the limiting beliefs we've carried," he explains, carefully placing it into your palm. "It embodies doubts, fears, shame—all things we've believed about ourselves were never truly ours."

He steps back slightly, allowing you a clear path to the Forge, his voice steady and encouraging. "When you're ready, cast this into the fire. Release these limiting beliefs clearly, fully. Watch as the flames accept them, transforming them from burdens into strength."

You move closer, feeling the heat of the flame—warm, inviting, cleansing. With intention and courage, you toss the tarnished metal into the heart of the flame. Instantly, the fire flares brilliantly, golden sparks erupting upward like stars, their glow dancing across your face. Slowly, the fire settles, revealing something gleaming beautifully within its heart—a piece of refined metal, shining brightly, purified and renewed.

Ardyn carefully retrieves the new piece from the flames, holding it out for you to take. Its surface gleams with clarity and strength.

"Now," he says softly, "you're ready to forge your mission. This refined piece symbolizes your potential, your clarity, your new belief. With it, we'll create a statement of purpose—a weapon your Moyux cannot withstand."

He guides you back toward the table with gentle, respectful encouragement, placing the refined metal in front of you along with fresh parchment.

"Write clearly, powerfully, and boldly. Transform your limiting beliefs into empowering truths—forge your mission statement, your greatest weapon."

He steps back gently, his presence quietly supportive, as you begin to write with newfound clarity and strength.

Journal Prompt II

From that empowered state, complete this mission statement: "I choose to become the one who _____, so that I may _____." *(Purpose: This anchors the identity shift and turns it into a vow, a sword, a spell—something declarative.)* Example:

- "I choose to become the one who speaks, even when my voice shakes, so that I may break the silence for others still unheard."

- "I choose to become the one who trusts their joy, so that I may lead others out of fear."

Arydn's voice guides you to the next step. *"If this mission were forged into a weapon, what would it look like? A sword, shield, staff, or torch? What materials would it be made of? What would its name be? Write your answers down in your journal."*

Forging Your Mission— The Flame of Renewal

Once done, Ardyn guides you to another sturdy wooden table beside the magical Forge. Spread across it is an impressive array of weapon molds, carefully crafted, intricate, and distinct. Each represents something unique, a symbolic embodiment of personal power and purpose.

"Every warrior requires a weapon uniquely suited to their battle," he explains. "Your weapon is not just symbolic—it embodies your new truths, your mission statement, crafted specifically to confront and overcome the unique challenges of your Moyux."

He gestures toward the molds, clearly and respectfully describing their symbolic significance:

- **Daggers** symbolize decisive action.

- **Swords** represent courage and bravery.

- **Shields** represent clear boundaries and resilience.

- **Maces and Hammers** embody decisive strength and assertiveness.

- **Staves** symbolize wisdom and self-worth.

- **Wands** embody clear intention, creativity, and personal influence.

- **Bows** represent focus and precision toward your goals.

- **Axes** represent courage to clear away self-doubt and obstacles.

Ardyn meets your gaze warmly, clearly encouraging. "Consider your Moyux carefully. Your weapon should clearly transform your vulnerabilities into powerful strengths. For example,

- "If your Moyux is rooted in self-doubt, craft a **Staff of Self-Dignity**, reminding you clearly and always of your worth.

- "If it feeds on fears of rejection, forge a **Shield of Self-Acceptance**, a constant reminder of your inherent worth beyond others' judgments.

- "If your challenge is hesitation or fear of action, select a **Sword of Decisiveness**, embodying courage and clear action."

Ardyn reaches for parchment nearby, tracing elegantly crafted sigils—symbols designed specifically to represent powerful, empowering beliefs.

"You've reshaped your limiting beliefs into new truths," he continues clearly. "Now, embed those truths within your chosen mold by selecting sigils that resonate deeply and embody your mission statement."

He demonstrates carefully, pressing each symbol into position with intention. "These sigils will transfer your empowering truths into the metal itself, embedding your weapon with purpose, resilience, and power."

He then goes on to summarize the process, ensuring you fully understand the importance of each step: "Choose your weapon mold clearly based on the strength you most need. Select sigils directly representing your empowering beliefs. Embed your transformed truths firmly into the mold, then place it into the Forge, knowing the flames will seal your new resolve permanently."

He steps back gently, respectful yet eager. "This weapon you craft symbolizes your transformation. As your weapon takes shape in the Forge, feel deeply that you're releasing old beliefs, replacing them with truths you've courageously chosen. In this moment, you are not only crafting your weapon—you're crafting your future." Ardyn nods encouragingly. "Forge your truth clearly and bravely, Seeker. This is your moment."

Interactive Activity: The Weapon Forging Ritual

Using what you already wrote in Chapter 5, Journal Prompts I and II,

1. **Face the Voice**
   If your Moyux could speak, what would it say to keep you small?
   "Don't _____, because _____."

What does that voice *fear* would happen if you grew beyond it?
It believes if I grow, I will...
Now ask: Whose voice might this be echoing from your past?
Does it sound like someone I once knew or a younger part of me?

2. **Reveal the Opposite**
   Imagine standing tall, unshaken, in front of your Moyux. Its power weakens in the presence of your truth.
   What is the opposite energy, the antidote, it cannot stand?
   The opposite of my Moyux is: (e.g., Boldness, Belonging, Joy, Expression)
   I have felt this power before when I...
   Let that memory return to you fully.
   Where were you? What did it feel like in your body?
   In that moment, I felt...

3. **Forge the Mission Statement**
   From this place of truth and strength, speak your vow into form:
   "I choose to become the one who

   _____

   so that I may

   _____**."**

   This is not just a sentence. It is a spell. An inscription. A beacon.

Purpose:

To vividly embody your transformational experience by creating a personal, tangible reminder of your Mission Statement—a symbolic weapon against your Moyux.

Instructions

Step 1: Choose or Create Your Symbolic Object

- Select or create a small physical item that symbolizes your chosen weapon.
  (Examples: A stick for a Staff, a stone for a Shield, a feather for a Wand, etc.)

- Clearly visualize this weapon embodying your strength and resolve.

Step 2: Empowering Inscription

- Write your empowering Mission Statement clearly and intentionally on paper. Fold it carefully to attach or tuck beneath your symbolic weapon.

Step 3: Symbolic Sigils

- Draw simple symbols (sigils) on a separate piece of paper clearly representing your new empowering beliefs.

- *(Optional: Reference mythology, nature, or create symbols uniquely personal to you.)*

Step 4: Ritual of Forging

- In a quiet, safe space, place your symbolic item, folded Mission Statement, and sigils before you.

- Light a candle or safely contain a small flame representing your transformative Forge.
  (Clearly visualize this flame if fire isn't available.)

- Boldly say your Mission Statement aloud, firmly feeling its truth resonate.

Step 5: Sealing Your Intention

- Carefully pass your symbolic item above the flame (or visualize clearly), affirming aloud:

    "I release my old beliefs, transforming them into strength, clarity, and courage. This weapon symbolizes my power, purpose, and readiness to face and overcome my Moyux."

- Attach or tuck your Mission Statement and sigils beneath your symbolic weapon, sealing your intentions clearly.

Step 6: Display Your Symbol

- Place your symbolic weapon clearly in your personal space, serving as a visible reminder of your commitment and transformation.

Step 7: Reflect and Affirm

- Hold your symbolic weapon gently. Clearly reflect on the significance of this transformation, affirming quietly:

    "I honor this transformation. I am ready to wield this power fully and bravely."

Note

- Visualize each step vividly if physical items are unavailable.

- Customize this ritual clearly and creatively to fit your personal style, beliefs, or imagination.

CHAPTER 6:
GATHERING MOMENTUM

The air has changed.

You sense it immediately—an electric current vibrating gently beneath your feet, resonating quietly through the deck of the *Aetherforge*. Around you, the skies deepen to shades of stormy indigo, clouds swirling rhythmically, forming patterns that almost feel intentional. Wind brushes softly against your face, sharper now, carrying an anticipatory chill as it slips through your fingers like whispers of the unknown.

You're close now.

Close to the heart of the Realm of Reflection.

Close to confronting your Moyux.

You glance down instinctively at your symbolic weapon—the tangible manifestation of your carefully forged truths and the mission statement you've courageously created. It gleams softly in your hand, imbued clearly with intention, purpose, and determination.

"Impressive," comes a familiar, warmly confident voice behind you.

You turn to see Eric leaning casually against the railing, amber eyes carefully studying you with gentle curiosity. He smiles reassuringly, nodding toward your weapon. "I can feel it from here—the strength, the purpose you've put into that."

He steps closer, joining you at the railing. His eyes scan the storm clouds thoughtfully, almost respectfully. "Do you sense it? How the Realm reacts to you? It's no accident. Your emotions, your resolve, your courage—they shape the path before you. Right now, the Realm knows you're here, and it's preparing as much as you are."

He pauses thoughtfully, his expression softening with sincerity. "It's natural to feel uncertainty here. Facing a Moyux is never easy. Truth is, many who come this far turn away right before the end. They fear failure, mistakes, setbacks, vulnerability."

His gaze meets yours firmly, gentle yet unyielding. "But mistakes and failures aren't something to fear. They're something to embrace. Growth doesn't happen in the absence of struggle—it happens because of it. If you stumble, and you likely will, just remember this: Every hero stumbles, even those who are trying to rescue themselves."

A quiet moment hangs between you, the words settling deep in your chest. Eric gently places his hand on your shoulder, anchoring you clearly in the moment. "You've already shown immense courage just by choosing to come this far. That courage, that resilience, matters more than perfection. Your weapon isn't powerful because it's flawless; it's powerful because it's authentically yours."

He steps back, releasing his reassuring grip, giving you room to breathe, to think, to prepare yourself mentally. As if responding to your resolve, the ship beneath you pulses gently, a quiet, affirming rhythm echoing your heartbeat.

Nearby, the rest of the crew quietly prepares, each clearly feeling the intensity of the approaching moment. Zara gracefully moves among them, her presence soothing, offering quiet words of reassurance that help ease hidden tensions. Celeste stands at the bow, her serene posture clearly indicating deep meditation, visualizing the confrontation ahead.

Ardyn busies himself organizing supplies, his movements efficient and purposeful. Occasionally, he glances your way, clearly affirming with a silent nod that you are ready, more ready than you know.

Finn sits quietly off to the side, his strong presence grounding, observant eyes carefully tracking the crew's emotional states. He notices you watching and nods subtly, offering clear, unspoken encouragement.

Thalia energetically directs the final preparations, clearly coordinating the crew's combined efforts to ensure unity, strength, and readiness. Each interaction feels purposeful, intentional—clearly building collective momentum.

Kael approaches quietly, pausing respectfully beside you. His voice is gentle yet firm. "Take a moment for yourself," he advises softly. "Rest your mind. Calm your breathing. Remember, every step you've taken, every doubt you've confronted, every fear you've faced has led you here intentionally. You are prepared, even if you don't feel it fully yet."

You take a slow, deliberate breath, steadying your nerves, anchoring yourself clearly in this moment of readiness. Eric's words return softly to your mind, strengthening your resolve:

"Your courage matters more than perfection."

As the ship moves steadily closer to the stormy heart of the Realm, a new kind of calm washes over you—clarity in the face of uncertainty. The Realm is waiting. Your Moyux is waiting. But you are ready. You have your weapon, your truths, and your allies. Your journey toward the Mirror of Sovereignty and the Moyux guarding it is no longer uncertain. It is inevitable.

Crossing the Cusp of Change

The air shifts abruptly.

A low rumble vibrates through the deck of the *Aetherforge,* deep and primal—a warning. Every muscle in your body tightens instinctively, adrenaline coursing through your veins with electric intensity. The Realm is awakening to your approach, clearly sensing your intent to confront the Moyux.

Eric's eyes snap forward, alert, determined. "Brace yourselves!" he calls sharply, his voice cutting through the thickening tension. "This is resistance, proof that we're close!"

The sky ahead darkens rapidly, clouds twisting aggressively into fierce spirals of indigo and silver, surging like living beasts protecting hidden truths. Lightning cracks violently across the sky, briefly illuminating swirling shadows and hinting at something vast and foreboding ahead.

The ship jolts suddenly, lurching beneath your feet as turbulence violently grips the *Aetherforge.* You grab tightly to the railing, heart racing, eyes wide. The peaceful quiet of moments before shatters into vivid chaos—wind screaming, energy crackling, reality itself seemingly protesting your advance.

Ardyn shouts clearly above the roar of the storm, feet planted firmly despite the ship's violent shaking. "Hold fast! Resistance means you're challenging something deep and true! Push through!"

Around you, your crew moves decisively, clearly embodying their guiding principles under pressure. Zara steadies herself gracefully, calmly whispering words of reassurance, counteracting panic. Celeste's eyes shine fiercely, unwavering focus locked on the tempest ahead. Finn, grounded like stone, holds firmly, silently transmitting deep strength. Kael chants quietly, channeling calm amidst chaos, his magic gently weaving threads of stability. Thalia energetically rushes to secure gear and crew alike, shouting clear orders with decisive confidence.

Eric steps beside you, voice powerful, resonant, electrifying the stormy air. "Feel that resistance clearly! That discomfort, that turbulence—it's your greatest sign! Change is happening! Transformation isn't gentle—it roars, it shakes, it pushes back. This is proof that you're breaking free!"

The Moyux senses your approach—its powerful presence clearly radiating outward, manifesting as chaos. You sense its agitation, its desperate attempt to repel your advance. It fears your courage. It fears your resolve.

"Push through it!" Eric roars boldly, encouragingly. "Let the storm challenge you! Remember your mission, your truth, your courage!"

Thunder crashes violently, reverberating through your chest. Lightning flashes again—so close now it nearly blinds. The wind screams with increasing intensity, battering you fiercely, challenging your resolve. The entire Realm resists your determination, attempting to push you back, to scare you away, to test your courage. Yet, clearly and defiantly, you step forward. The weapon you've forged pulses fiercely in your hand, reflecting clearly your commitment, your clarity, your truth. This isn't just a storm—this is the physical manifestation of everything that's ever held you back. Fear. Doubt. Shame. Resistance. But, despite the fierce turbulence, despite your pounding heartbeat, you feel something undeniably strong rising within you:

Resolve.

Eric calls loudly again, voice ringing with vibrant energy: "Almost there! Stand strong!"

You look up and your breath catches sharply. Directly ahead, amidst swirling, chaotic clouds, the Core of Reflection emerges. At its center, pulsing powerfully, the Mirror of Sovereignty glows with intense clarity, guarded fiercely by the presence of your Moyux. Its energy unmistakable. Its roar deafening.

This is your turning point.

You feel fear, but beneath it lies something greater, something unstoppable:

Determination.

Your crew's presence pulses strongly around you, their collective strength reinforcing your resolve. Their courage, their unity, their clarity—they all amplify yours.

The *Aetherforge* bucks wildly, straining forward through the intensifying resistance, charging bravely into the storm's violent heart. This moment is the crucible, clearly testing the strength of your commitment, the depth of your courage.

Eric shouts over the chaos once more, voice ringing fiercely with fiery resolve:

"THIS IS IT! THIS IS YOUR MOMENT! CLAIM IT!"

The Realm roars louder—desperate, defiant, fearful of your strength. The Moyux's presence surges furiously ahead, energy exploding outward in waves of raw emotional power.

But you are ready. You've prepared clearly, deliberately, courageously.

And with your heart thundering defiantly—

With your soul ignited by unyielding clarity—

With your resolve blazing fiercely against all resistance—

You step forward decisively, embracing this moment, embracing transformation itself.

You have done it! You have crossed over into yet another threshold fully, defiantly, boldly—

And the storm itself roars in furious welcome.

CHAPTER 7:

ECHOES OF RESISTANCE,
THE FOG OF CERTAINTY &
THE ANCHOR OF FAMILIARITY

The storm behind you fades like a memory—loud, defiant, and suddenly distant. As the *Aetherforge* pushes beyond the edge of the maelstrom, the world around you stills unnaturally, as if the Realm itself holds its breath.

The light shifts. What was once chaos now gives way to something far stranger.

A dense fog creeps silently across the sky, curling like fingers around the hull of the *Aetherforge.* It's not the kind of mist that merely obscures sight—it *presses* against your mind, thick with presence, whispering things you can almost understand and yet dare not to. The further you drift into it, the more muffled the world becomes. Sound is swallowed. Shapes blur. Even your own thoughts begin to echo strangely in your mind.

Then—

A scream. Distant. Dissonant. Echoing from no clear direction.

Another follows. Then another—each one layered atop the last until the fog itself seems to *breathe* with the wailing of unseen souls. These aren't cries of pain alone. They're laced with confusion, doubt, and something more ancient. Something that *resists*.

Celeste grips the edge of the railing, her silver gaze glowing faintly as she peers through the murk. "I can see the Mirror of Sovereignty," she says quietly, "However everything between us and it… is cloaked. Like the path is hiding itself."

Eric narrows his eyes, his hand resting on the hilt of his blade. "Then we proceed with more than sight. Stay sharp."

Suddenly, the *Aetherforge* lurches—not from turbulence, but from something deeper. Something unseen is *pulling it back*. You look over the side and see the mist curling in tendrils along the hull—seeking purchase, like it *knows* who you are and what you intend.

Zara inhales sharply. "Something's wrong… this fog—"

"Is *alive*," Kael finishes grimly, his voice calm, even as his magic shimmers around him, ready for something.

Then it speaks.

A voice from the fog. Genderless. Ageless. Disembodied.

"You wish to see clearly? Then stop seeking so hard."

A figure takes form—half seen, half imagined—a guide cloaked in layers of translucent fog. It walks along the bow of the ship, head tilted, movements unnatural. "Answers demand silence. Stillness. However your minds…are… so … loud."

Eric steps forward. "Who are you?"

The figure smiles, though not a kind one. "I am *what you crave*, the Fog of Certainty," the guide whispers again, just before vanishing, "and I will thicken with every answer you demand." Before you can respond, the apparition dissolves into mist.

The compass on the *Aetherforge* begins to spin wildly. The controls no longer respond. Even the stars above flicker and shift like uncertain memories.

Kael frowns, brow furrowed. "The Fog of Certainty... it clouds more than vision. It clouds *choice.*"

You feel it. The pressure. The urge to demand answers, to *grasp* for control, to *force* direction. However the more you reach, the deeper you sink into confusion.

Then—another weight.

It hits your back like a memory and suddenly you're *wearing* it: a golden anchor chained to your shoulders, shimmering with familiar warmth. Your childhood room. A lover's touch. The first success you ever tasted. It feels *safe.* Comfortable. Why move forward when what you had was enough?

A second voice echoes—this one smooth, soothing, nostalgic.

"You've come far. Why risk what you've built? Stay here. Stay with what you know."

Another figure appears, this one cloaked in shimmering gold, their face shifting between loved ones and mentors long past. Their words stroke your fears like an old lullaby. "I am the Anchor of Familiarity," the golden figure murmurs, "and I shimmer with everything you've ever feared to lose."

Celeste shudders. *"The Anchor of Familiarity."*

"Loss aversion," Kael murmurs. "It pulls you back... with memories."

Illusions begin dancing across the ship—visions of lives you could return to. Paths abandoned. Loves lost. Homes forgotten. They glow warmly, seductively, calling the crew back from the edge of transformation.

You see some of your team falter. Even Finn, ever grounded, seems momentarily unsure.

Because now this is the test.

Two Echoes of Resistance—one clouding your vision with the *need* for clarity, the other weighing you down with the *fear* of letting go.

Ahead lies the truth. Only if you can *let go* of your need to see it all and bless what you've left behind.

The fog thickens. The illusions shimmer brighter. These weren't monsters of fang or flame. They were ideas—enticing ones—echoing the soft, familiar voices inside every Seeker who's ever hesitated at the edge of change.

You must decide: Do you listen to the voices that echo from within or trust the silence that waits beyond

A sudden *crack* of energy erupts across the deck.

Kael's voice rings out, louder than it should be, cutting through the illusions like lightning through mist. "Enough!" he shouts, his cloak billowing as raw magic begins to swirl around him in radiant currents of indigo and silver. His eyes blaze like twin moons, burning with arcane fire. He raises a hand and the air around him ripples. "These aren't just memories. They're chains! Fog to confuse you, anchors to hold you down! The path ahead isn't blocked by force—it's blocked by your own hesitation."

The fog resists him, curling closer, almost mocking.

"We're not done here," Kael growls. "But you—" His eyes lock onto you, fierce and steady. "You must *look inward* before we can strike outward. Name what still holds you. Name what still stops you. Only then will your power return to you."

He slams his staff to the deck. A pulse of light bursts outward. And in the space between that pulse and the fog's next whisper—

You feel it:

This isn't just preparation.

This is *initiation*.

Journal Prompt I

When was the last time you experienced resistance to change? Was it loud and defiant like a storm screaming "You're not ready!"? Or was it a quiet whispering, "Why bother? You already have enough..."?

Pause. Let the questions settle.

Now ask yourself:

1. What clarity or guarantee did you believe you needed before it was safe to take the first step?
   What were you trying to prove, avoid, or control and how did that shape your delay?

2. What part of your identity felt at risk the moment you chose to grow?
   Was it comfort, community, or a familiar role?
   What did you fear you'd lose and what deeper truth were you stepping toward?

3. If you gave more trust to the unknown, what door might have opened sooner?
   Imagine what could've shifted if you had listened to your future self instead of your fear.

4. Now, standing at this threshold: What becomes possible if you bless what was and listen to what is becoming? What part of you is whispering, "It's time"?
   Let this be a moment of release. Let this be your Liminal space to feel through.

Close your eyes. Breathe. Notice where resistance still clings.
And ask gently: *What if the fog is not here to stop me... but to teach me how to see differently? To challenge me to look at life from a different perspective?*

Declaring Your Renewal

The light from Kael's staff pulses once more and this time, the fog *screams* back in fury. The Realm has heard your reflection and it does not approve.

The illusions that once drifted gently across the deck now lash out. They twist. Sharpen. And *evolve* from posing as memories into movements like that of predators. They move with intent and hunger.

And then—a voice returns.

The Anchor's tone has shifted. No longer a whisper. A warning now.

"Turn back. This is your last chance."

The golden figure manifests at the bow of the ship—its glow unstable, flickering like flame ready to consume itself. Its once-kind face is hardened now, a mask of nostalgic menace. It steps forward slowly, eyes fixed on you.

"Why throw away everything you've built? Don't you remember how hard it was to get here?" Each word drips like honey laced with poison—so familiar, so warm, so *reasonable*. And then the fog condenses. Thick vapor rolls across the deck, crawling like a living thing. In moments, it coalesces into a tall figure of smoke and stillness. No features, just presence. Its voice slides into your mind like ice.

"You still don't know where you're going. You think reflection is strength; without direction, it's just wandering. You can't win this without clarity. And you have *none*."

The fog pulses violently.

The *Aetherforge* shudders beneath your feet.

The controls freeze.

The compass spins.

The sky above blurs and bends like a reflection in broken glass.

Every sound begins to echo—too loud, too long.

Your own breath comes back at you in fragments.

And that's when the crew begins to fracture.

Zara falters first. Her hand trembles as she reaches for a vision shimmering off the starboard side—her childhood home, sunlight pouring through the trees. A door opens. Someone she loves is there, smiling. Her voice cracks. "It feels so real..."

Finn stumbles, eyes locked on an illusion unfolding before him. There, in golden light, is a version of himself, *resting.* A life of peace. No missions. No weight on his shoulders. No constant need to hold the world steady. For a breath, he leans toward it.

Even **Eric's** jaw clenches tight. He grips the railing like it's the only thing holding him here. His knuckles whiten, and yet he doesn't speak. But the pull on him is clear, as if part of him remembers who he was *before* this fight. Before the truth.

The illusions are no longer passive. They are *personal.*

Tailored.

Targeted.

And terrifyingly *believable.*

The ship groans under the weight of emotional gravity.

Then, a spark.

Kael steps forward. His staff rises, and with it, the swirling currents of his magic ignite—spirals of starlight and shadow spinning around his limbs. His cloak flares outward as the winds respond to *him.* His eyes blaze with radiant focus.

"No more!" Kael shouts, voice echoing across the deck like thunder made from truth. "These are not guardians. They are ghosts. And they only live because *we* feed them."

The Fog curls tighter around the *Aetherforge*, trying to snuff out the rising energy, but Kael's aura pushes back.

"They speak in your voice," he calls, stepping to the center of the ship. "They wear the faces you long to see. Even so they are *not real.*" He slams his staff into the deck. A ring of silver-blue energy bursts outward, washing over the crew, rattling the illusions, distorting their forms.

The golden figure falters, its mask flickering. The warm voice of the Anchor becomes unsteady. "You're tired..." It tries again, "You've earned rest, haven't you?"

Even so Kael isn't alone now.

Celeste steps beside him, lowering her blades, glowing with a quiet celestial aura. "Let the fog lie," she growls. "We move forward *because* we're uncertain. That's where trust lives."

Zara, eyes still glistening, closes her hand into a fist. She breathes deeply and steps back from the illusion of her sister. "I miss you," she whispers, voice steady. "Despite this, I won't stay frozen in yesterday."

Finn exhales slowly. His illusion tries one last trick—offers him the warmth of peace—except he shakes his head. "Rest can wait," he mutters. "There's work left to do."

Thalia moves quickly now, grabbing Zara's hand. "We didn't fight this far to fall asleep in dreams. We *build* what comes next. We don't run back to what was."

Ardyn pulls out his blades from his black leather belt, igniting them with his fire magic and swipes vigorously at his illusions as it laughs and mocks his attempts to harm it. "I have better use of my fire anywhere, without needing to do it here."

And then Eric, finally, speaks. He steps forward, voice low but iron-solid. "Enough coddling. Enough confusion." He turns to you. "This is your moment, Seeker. Not theirs, but *Yours.*"

Kael's magic coils upward in a spiral, rising high above the deck like a beacon. "Now!" he shouts, power crescendoing. "Seeker—speak it! Declare what you choose! Say it *aloud!*"

The Realm shudders.

The Fog swirls wildly, desperate to drown the light. The Anchor flickers, its chains glowing with final intensity.

And you—

You step forward.

The illusions press in louder.

Eric steps towards you. He doesn't say much. Just offers you a scroll, neatly rolled and bound with a thin silver ribbon. He places it into your hands with quiet certainty. "I knew you would," he says, his voice warm and steady. "When you are ready."

You look at him—his eyes filled with *recognition*. He knows how far you've come. He knows what this moment means.

You unroll the scroll. Its ink shimmers faintly, as if the words were written by the Realm itself.

And as your eyes move across the lines, something deep within you responds. This isn't just something to read.

It's something to *remember*.

Your Declaration of Renewal

I release the echoes that no longer define me.
I honor what I've survived and what I've outgrown.
I call back my energy from every place I left myself behind.
I reclaim my voice, my vision, and my vibration.
I choose clarity over confusion, courage over fear, presence over perfection.
From this moment forward, I walk in alignment with my truth.
I open myself to new growth, new embodiment, and new mastery.
I am not who I was...
I am who I choose to become.

You raise your voice into the deep spaces *within* where these Echoes have lived the longest.

The fog collapses into vapor, the final scream of resistance fading into the silence that follows truth. The golden Anchor shatters in reverence. It breaks like a story that has reached its final line, its ending understood. Its pieces shimmer upward and vanish like wishes returned to the stars.

The deck stills.

The mist withdraws.

The sky begins to clear.

But before anyone speaks—

The scroll glows faintly as the final line settles into your heart, like a seed finding its soil.

You look up.

Zara's hand rests over her chest.

Celeste closes her eyes, lips parted in silent reverence.

Thalia smiles—open, unguarded.

Kael's gaze is steady, proud.

Even the *Aetherforge* seems quieter now—lighter, as if breathing with you.

Eric places a hand on your shoulder. "Keep that with you. Not just the scroll—" He taps two fingers gently against your heart. "*That.*"

You nod.

The illusions are gone.

The trial is behind you.

And yet, something ahead calls even more deeply.

The Cloak of Thorns

The *Aetherforge* slows. It hums softly beneath your feet, as if exhaling in surrender. Ahead, the sky peels back to reveal a vast, spiraling descent—a crater of mirrored terrain, layered in light and shadow. Pools of glasslike water stretch across the landscape, reflecting *you*. Shards of crystal float silently in the air, drifting like forgotten thoughts waiting to be remembered.

Eric stands at the helm, hands resting gently on the controls. He doesn't force the ship forward. He simply says, "This is where we walk."

Kael steps beside him, already forming a glowing sigil in the air—a portal of shifting silver and indigo. "The *Aetherforge* wasn't meant to enter what's next," he says softly. "This is a path that must be taken... with feet on the ground and truth in the body."

One by one, the crew gathers at the portal. You feel the air shift as you step through. And then, you noticed it. The ground here doesn't feel solid. It feels like memory. Every step you take ripples outward across the mirrored pools beneath your feet, distorting your reflection before snapping it back into place. You don't cast a single reflection—you cast many.

Each one flickers with a different expression. A different version of you.

Celeste scans the horizon, blades drawn. "This place sees *everything*."

Zara's eyes are wide. "It's beautiful... however I don't trust it."

Kael murmurs, "Not all protection is love. Some of it is fear with wrapped intentions."

That's when you feel it.

A presence—subtle, silken yet familiar.

A soft voice curls around your spine like velvet and wire.

"You don't have to keep going."

The words drift through the air like falling petals—gentle, weightless, almost kind.

Something in your body reacts before your mind does. A tightening in your chest. A stilling of breath. That voice. It doesn't shout. It doesn't threaten.

It *reminds you.*

Of every time you nearly broke.

Of every moment you considered stopping from exhaustion.

A figure steps slowly from behind one of the floating crystal shards. They wear a long, embroidered cloak—deep navy and dusk-gold, elegant in its craftsmanship. It shimmers like memory, moves like forgiveness. For a moment, you feel drawn to it. Safe. Wrapped. Forgotten. Yet with each soft step forward, the illusion wavers. The fabric of the cloak twists. Tightens. Folds in on itself.

And you see them now—**thorns**, hidden beneath the woven brilliance. Sharp. Barbed. Perfectly positioned to dig deeper the more you move. The figure's face is warm. Familiar, somehow. Like someone you once trusted deeply and yet can't quite place. Their voice flows like calm water over wounds that haven't fully healed.

"You've done enough," they say, a note of sympathy in every syllable. "There's no shame in resting here. No danger. No disappointment. Only peace."

The mirrored pools beneath your feet shimmer as they speak, flickering with images: moments when things fell apart. Times you tried and failed. Times you rose and were cut down. Every failure etched in silver, swirling just beneath the surface.

The figure moves closer.

"Why push forward when you already hurt so much?" They tilt their head slightly. "Haven't you proven enough?"

Your reflection in the pools begins to fracture again from the tension building inside you.

Kael's voice cuts through the stillness, low yet firm. "The Cloak of Thorns."

The figure's eyes flick toward him, yet they don't flinch.

Instead, they reach out, running one hand gently along the edge of their cloak, subtly hiding the thorns. "I'm not your enemy.

I'm here to protect what's left of you." Their fingers brush the embroidery with reverence. "You've bled enough."

Zara steps back a pace, hand drifting toward her satchel. Her voice trembles. "It's not threatening us. It's... *cradling* us."

Celeste exhales slowly. "That's worse."

The Cloak of Thorns spreads their arms, like a guardian offering sanctuary. "Stay here and you won't have to be brave anymore."

And with that, the Realm shifts again. The air becomes heavier, thicker with sensation. Each movement, no matter how small, sends a dull sting across your skin, like memory turned to thorn.

Thalia winces, grabbing their forearm. "What is this—?"

Kael closes his eyes, jaw tightening. "It's not a curse. It's *overprotection with discouragement,* a form of resistance to keep us from proceeding further. These thorns... they're the echoes of every time you told yourself it was safer or okay to not try again."

Ardyn lowers his blades slightly, staring into the nearest pool. "It doesn't want to fight. It wants to *convince.*"

The figure smiles. "You've come far. Farther than most. Isn't that enough?"

The mirrored ground ripples with each word, reflecting the subtle truth behind the voice: *Safety that costs your growth. Protection that demands your stagnation.*

And still, the cloak glimmers. Beautiful. Enticing.

Something inside you... remembers.

That rest is sacred.

The mirrored ground beneath you hums, pulsing in rhythm with the Cloak's voice.

Its presence isn't louder, it's *closer.* More intimate.

Every word seeps into the folds of memory, tracing the old aches you thought you'd outgrown.

And Kael lets out a shout. It was one of pain as he begins to falter. His shoulders draw inward, just slightly. You notice it. The usual grace in his posture breaks. His staff, always steady, trembles faintly in his grip. He lifts it, gathering energy into a pale glow. However, the spell falters. The sigil dissolves mid-air, unraveling like thread torn from fraying cloth. He blinks hard, shaking his head. "No... this is projection... I *know* what this is."

The Cloak steps closer, gaze fixed not on Kael's strength but on his hesitation.

"Your power asks so much of you," it says gently. "Wouldn't it be easier to put it down? Just for a while?"

Kael's breath grows shallow. The thorns seem to tighten invisibly around his chest.

Zara acts quickly. She reaches into her satchel, whispering under her breath. Illusion magic begins to shimmer in the air—golden threads weaving through light and shadow, creating shifting mirages that encircle the Cloak.

A burst of fog. A wall of fire. A fractured sky. All at once.

"Leave him alone!" Zara's voice cracks with emotion. "Go! You're not real! You're just a story made of fear *and we are done listening to you!*"

Yet the Cloak does not flinch.

The illusions fade against its calm, radiant stillness. It doesn't strike back—it *absorbs*, like a thick blanket smothering sparks.

Zara gasps, her magic draining as fast as she weaves it.

Kael drops to one knee.

He grips the ground with one hand, the other pressed to his chest. "I've seen this before... this feeling. Like something wrapping around the soul, whispering, 'Don't risk it.' It's not malice. It's memory."

His voice is shaking.

"I'm sorry," he whispers. "I... I can't hold it this time."

And that's when Thalia steps forward. Her movement is fast, instinctive and *devotional*. She drops to one knee beside him and grabs his shoulders. "Kael. Look at me."

He doesn't. His eyes are glazed, distant. She grips tighter.

"*Kael.* You told me—when the ground feels like memory, press your feet into it and remind it who you are."

His lips part, trembling. "I can't feel my anchor."

"Then use *mine*."

She places her forehead to his. "You are more than what you protect. You are not your past pain. You are the reason we're still standing."

His hands tremble in hers.

Then, slowly, light flickers in his palms.

Not summoned—*remembered*.

Kael exhales, grounding. His magic doesn't blaze—it *settles*, forming a pulse of soft silver that begins to shield the others.

"Thank you," he murmurs. "I needed someone to see me through."

The Cloak tilts its head, eyes narrowing.

Before it can step forward, Finn moves.

Quiet. Focused. Purposeful.

He kneels by the nearest reflective pool, cups his hands, and lifts a splash of mirrored water, throwing it directly onto the Cloak's embroidered fabric.

The effect is immediate.

The area touched by water sizzles faintly, the embroidery unraveling in slow, silver strands. The illusion buckles, twisting in on itself.

Finn doesn't speak. He just keeps throwing water, again and again. Each splash dissolves a bit more of the charm, revealing the thorns beneath. Real. Sharp. No longer hidden by care. The Cloak snarls in panic. It's being *seen*.

Eric steps forward now, eyes burning. He draws his blade to *command*. "Leave them!" he shouts, voice ringing with force. "You have no power here anymore!"

However the blade does nothing. The Cloak merely glances at him, then turns away, untouched.

It was never fighting with blades.

It was fighting with memory.

Eric lowers his weapon slowly, the truth dawning. "This isn't my battle to win..."

You feel it too.

This is not a war of force.

It is a choice.

The Cloak's voice hangs in the air, delicate as a web, and just as dangerous. "Are you ready to risk everything you've protected... for something you haven't yet become?"

The question doesn't strike like a weapon.

It *settles*, like ash.

Soft. Slow. Unshakable.

For a moment, no one speaks.

The air is thick with memory, with longing, with the ache of all you've carried to survive.

Then—

Celeste steps forward with her hands open—palms offered to the sky, as if baring her soul to the wind. Her voice rises, quiet, unwavering. A truth that doesn't need volume to be heard.

"Letting go isn't loss," she says. "It's choosing to stop carrying what was never meant to come with you." She looks to you, and her gaze is luminous. Alive and filled with *recognition*. She sees the part of you still curled inward, still afraid to loosen your grip. "Safety can't carry your sovereignty," she says, her voice trembling with care. "And protection without purpose becomes a prison lined with soft words and thorned walls."

You feel it. The slow unraveling of something tight in your chest. The Cloak shudders from the slow erosion of its illusion.

Then—

Ardyn steps forward. His presence is weight and warmth, like sunlight on stone. He moves with the patience of someone who has lived through storms and still believes in spring. His voice is low. Steady. Rooted.

"There comes a time," he says, "when what once saved you... starts to silence you." He pauses, the silence reverent. Then his eyes, kind, unwavering, settle on you. "This is that time."

A breath.

"We're not asking you to abandon yourself," he continues, stepping closer. **"We're asking you to *return* to yourself. The version of you that doesn't have to shrink to survive."**

His words settle like sacred soil, making space for something new to root.

A hush falls over the mirrored field.

Celeste turns to you once more, her voice softer now. An invocation. **"Let it go, not because it failed but because you are ready to grow beyond it."**

Journal Prompt II: Pressure of Protection

Let the stillness settle around and *within* you. Then ask yourself— *with compassion, not judgment*:

1. What part of me still believes I need this protection and what is it afraid would happen if I let it go?
   Is this protection fear, control, perfection, overgiving, or silence? *Whose voice does it echo? And what has it been trying to shield me from?*

2. If I gently released this protection, what power, presence, or gift might begin to return to me naturally?

What qualities of mine have been waiting patiently beneath the surface?

What does my truth sound like when it's no longer filtered through fear?

Relinquishing the Bind

The Cloak lowers its arms. No resistance. No flourish. Only resignation. Its shimmering fabric begins to loosen at the shoulders, slipping down like water losing form. The magic holding it together begins to fray. Threads unwind, embroidery unravel into soft, sagging folds.

And then—

Kael stumbles forward, gasping.

The invisible thorns around his chest fall away in brittle, curling strands. His staff clatters gently against the ground, untouched by threat—only by weight.

Thalia is at his side in an instant, arms bracing him, forehead to his.

"I'm here," she whispers. "I've got you."

Kael's eyes are still unfocused because his tears pool quietly beneath his lashes. He exhales like someone who's just woken from a dream that lasted too long.

"It made a home in my silence," he murmurs. "Wrapped its thorns around my stillness and called it peace."

Thalia doesn't reply. She just holds him.

The Cloak slowly lowers to its knees out of *exhaustion*.

And then you see it.

Where the garment once shimmered with dignity and grace, now only raw truth remains. The Cloak peels back, exposing what it had always hidden:

A heart.

Suspended in a twisted lattice of black vines and jagged thorns, pulsing slow and uneven.

Ink-dark secretion, bleeding out slow tendrils of thick, toxic memory. It spills across the mirrored floor like grief that never found voice—coiling into the pools, staining their reflections.

The Seeker in the water no longer looks back at you. They just wait.

Quietly.

For release.

The Cloak lifts its tired gaze.

"You've outgrown me." The voice is almost tender now. Almost... grateful. "I only ever wanted to keep you safe," it murmurs. "And I did. For a while. Nevertheless **safety... is not the same as freedom."**

And then it begins to dissolve. Piece by piece, it slips backward into the nearest mirrored pool. The vines retract. The threads unweave. The bleeding heart unhooks itself from the thorns and falls gently into the water, rippling once, then vanishing beneath the surface.

Just before it disappears completely, its eyes meet yours one last time.

"You'll call for me again. Not because you want to... but because you'll hurt again. And I'll still be here. To embrace you once again like we have always done before."

Just the promise of pain remembered.

Then it is gone.

The water stills.

No reflection remains—only the faint glimmer of light returning to the surface.

Kael slowly straightens, supported by Thalia, breath steadier now. His magic no longer flares—it simply glows, soft and constant.

"I see it clearly now," he says. "The part of me that thought silence was the safest way to survive." He closes his eyes. "And I release it."

Eric watches with quiet reverence, saying nothing. He doesn't need to.

Celeste turns toward you with understanding.

"You didn't destroy it," she says. "You unwrapped it and you know its intentions no matter whose face is hiding it."

The Realm is still.

There's more space now.

More breath.

More truth.

You haven't just passed a test.

You've laid something down—something heavy, something old.

And in its place, something new stirs in the distance.

Kael exhales, steadying himself as the last traces of shadow dissolve beneath the mirrored surface.

"Well," he says, voice a little hoarse, yet tinged with dry relief, "that was definitely the Cloak of Thorns." He looks around slowly, catching his breath. **"Which means we've now faced three Echoes of Resistance, and..."**

Finn finishes the sentence for him, his voice quiet, resolute—each word like a stone dropped into still water: **"Two more to go."**

The Realm falls silent again. However, the silence is different now. It feels like space—cleared, sacred and waiting.

Within you.

Around you.

Ahead of you.

The journey is not over.

Nonetheless something essential has already shifted.

Healing the Healer

Kael walks slowly now—slower than before. His shoulders, always poised, slope forward slightly, the weight of unseen wounds pressing into him. Each step leaves a subtle imprint across the mirrored ground, not in dust or shadow, only in silence. He lowers to one knee. His breath catches from the quiet ache of being *seen* in his unraveling.

You approach without words.

The crew, sensing the depth of what stirs between you, falls into a gentle stillness.

Kael lifts his gaze to meet yours. His eyes, always calm, are luminous now with quiet need.

"I've healed many," he says, his voice edged with something soft and breaking. "I've woven light into the broken, held pain without flinching. However this—" he gestures faintly to his own chest, where the remnants of the Cloak's thorns still linger in unseen places, "—this reached somewhere I cannot reach alone."

He closes his eyes, a small tremor in his hands. "I forgot," he breathes. "Even the strongest healers need someone else to remind them who they are." His hands open, palms turned upward. "I know I can heal. And yet I also know I'm not meant to do this alone."

A pause.

Then, with reverent clarity:

"Your Declaration... it wasn't just forged to strike down resistance. It is a living force. A spell made from sovereignty. From memory. From truth." His voice softens. "It can destroy what harms and it can also restore what was damaged." He lowers his hands to his knees and bows his head, fully open now. "If you're ready... call me back."

And in that moment, the invitation isn't made to power. It's made to *presence*.

You step closer.

You don't speak.

You *remember*.

You close your eyes to listen. To the part of you that has always known how to return light to the places it was lost.

And in that stillness, something begins to stir from within.

Your Declaration of Renewal

I release the echoes that no longer define me.
I honor what I've survived and what I've outgrown.
I call back my energy from every place I left myself behind.
I reclaim my voice, my vision, and my vibration.
I choose clarity over confusion, courage over fear, presence over perfection.
From this moment forward, I walk in alignment with my truth.
I open myself to new growth, new embodiment, and new mastery.
I am not who I was...
I am who I choose to become.

It rises as memory, as clarity, as choice.

A warmth gathers whole. Intentional. Alive. The Declaration lives again, embodied in the form of healing.

Zara exhales, her hand pressing gently to her heart. Thalia steps beside her, their hand finding Zara's, eyes wide with wonder. No words pass between them—their silence says everything.

Finn stands just behind you, steady as ever, a mountain of quiet reverence.

Eric crosses his arms with a half-smile, pride and recognition shining in his eyes.

"You were never meant to follow," he says. "You were meant to *rise*."

The light reaches Kael like sunlight slipping into a shuttered room. It touches his chest. His hands. His breath. He lifts his face slightly—eyes fluttering open—and lets the healing move through him. Just allowing. The glow settles into his skin like a returning memory.

"I remember now," he whispers. "Healing isn't about being invincible... it's about trusting someone enough to let them *see you hurting*." He places a hand over his heart where the light still lingers. "And I receive it."

Slowly, Kael rises whole in a way he hadn't been before.

Ardyn steps forward, arms crossed, fire sparking faintly in his palm. His voice is rough with pride.

"Well then," he says. "You've got a weapon forged from truth, and the fire of a Seer in your chest. I'd say you're ready."

The crew falls in line beside you, no longer guiding—now walking *with* you.

The cavern looms just ahead. Dark. Silent. Sacred.

Two final Echoes wait beyond the borderland—

Echoes born from how the world once made you fear *yourself*.

Despite this you do not approach them empty. You walk forward whole.

Celeste steps forward first, her eyes distant, gazing through the path ahead. She raises her hand to the sky, fingers catching the faint glimmer of starlight breaking through the mist above. Her voice is soft. "They're aligning," she says. "The stars. The route forward reveals itself only when we trust what we can't yet see."

Beside her, Finn kneels, his hand pressed against the earth. He closes his eyes, listening for a *shift*. A long pause. Then a single, quiet word:

"Left."

Celeste nods. "Agreed."

Eric glances between them and smiles faintly. "Sky and stone. Never wrong when they speak together."

No more words are needed. The crew follows, guided by attunement.

Celeste walks like wind over water, navigating through intuition and ancestral memory.

Finn moves like the forest itself—deliberate, grounded, deeply listening.

The path begins to curve downward. The terrain shifts, narrowing. Air thickens.

And then—

You arrive.

The Shackles of Silence & The Mirror of Shadows

The cavern entrance stands wide and dark before you, hewn by time itself. Jagged stone arches curve into shadow, pulsing faintly with something alive. Beneath your feet, the ground vibrates with a heartbeat not your own.

Celeste halts, breath held.

Finn straightens slowly, jaw clenched.

At the point of no return, a presence waits.

A tall, jagged structure rises just within the mouth of the cavern—a reflecting stone, twisted and towering, like a shard of darkness carved from the spine of the earth itself.

It is the Mirror of Shadows.

Its surface is not smooth—it undulates softly, like liquid memory beneath glass. You can't see your reflection. Only movement. Only *others.*

And then—

Light rises.

Without warning, a veil of white light extends from the ground, enclosing each of you in a vertical, glowing pillar.

The crew calls out—each of them muffled, visible but unreachable. Even the ground no longer responds to your movement. You are *held suspended* upwards above the ground.

Inside your cell of light, the Mirror of Shadows changes.

It begins to twist, swirl, and then—

a **face** forms.

However, it is not yours.

The face has no eyes. Only a mouth. It opens unnaturally wide and begins to speak.

Not in your voice.

It's in **the voices of others**.

"You'll never be enough."

"You always ruin everything."

"No one will ever truly love you."

"You're too much."

"You're not enough."

"This is all your fault."

"You should be ashamed."

"Why can't you just be normal?"

"Everything falls apart because of you."

"You're weak."

"You're broken."

"You don't matter."

The voice is not cruel—it is **indifferent**. Mechanical. Rehearsed.

A projection machine, running the same script again and again.

You feel your breath shorten. The words slip into you like old smoke, familiar and cold.

The light around you begins to pulse—reacting to your heartbeat, to your memory, to the weight of each phrase.

The Mirror of Shadows does not shout.

It does not rage.

It **reflects**.

Yet at the same time, it's what you've been told to believe.

This is not a battle of fire or blade.

This is a battle of *definition*.

You stand now on the edge of your sovereignty, facing every voice that ever tried to name you without knowing who you truly are.

And somewhere in the silence behind those words...

Your truth waits to rise.

The Mirror hums—low and rhythmic, like a spell spoken a thousand times too many.

"You never change."

"You'll never be strong enough."

"You should just give up."

Each word sinks in like **gravity**. It's **Pressure.**

You feel it pull at your breath, your spine, the muscles just beneath your ribs. Not because you believe it but because, once, **you did**.

And then—

Eric's voice rips through the stillness like a flare in the fog. **"Shackles of Silence!"** he shouts, eyes narrowing. He pounds his fist against the pillar of white light that surrounds him. "They're not just showing us shame—they're *silencing* us. Making us believe we don't get to speak back."

The white veil hums around him, suppressing the echo of his voice.

Celeste reaches outward, her hands glowing with Starfire—yet the magic doesn't leave her fingertips. **"It's learned helplessness,"** she says, breath tight. "A prison you stop trying to leave because you've forgotten how."

Zara's eyes widen as the full shape of the trap comes into view. **"They're working together,"** she breathes. She presses both palms to the glowing wall around her, voice rising. **"The Mirror and the Shackles—they're not separate. One steals your voice. The other replaces it with poison."**

The Mirror's mouth twists—with continuation.

"They only pretend to care."

"You're too sensitive."

"You're a burden."

Across the chamber, **Finn doesn't move.** His eyes are fixed on the Mirror

The words keep coming.

"You're weak."

"You'll never measure up."

"They're only nice to you because they pity you."

Finn's hands hang at his sides. Then, very slowly, his jaw tightens. His breath sharpens. His shoulders rise in *remembrance.* The silence around him begins to **strain.**

And then, he speaks.

"I know these words." His voice is low. Steady. Each syllable sounds like it's being pulled from somewhere deep and buried. **"I carried them once. Thought they were mine."** He lifts his eyes to the Mirror. His voice grows louder, cracking from *truth breaking open.* "I let them name me. I let them quiet me." His fists curl now, pressed against the inside of the light. "I kept showing up. I held others when I was breaking. I listened when no one else did."

The veil around him trembles, thin cracks of silver light forming at his palms. **"That's not weakness."** His voice booms now, echoing into the stone. **"That's compassion. That's power."**

The veil of light expands outward from him, *stretching*, like truth pushing through old lies.

Zara presses her fist to her lips, tears shining in her eyes. She doesn't speak. She doesn't need to.

Thalia bows their head slightly, hand pressed over their chest like they're holding something sacred.

Eric watches, something fierce and proud burning behind his eyes. "He's not just speaking back," he mutters. "He's *rewriting the silence.*"

The Mirror of Shadows ripples. The face distorts. The mouth falters.

No rage. Just... a pause.

Recognition of something it cannot erase: Truth, spoken with strength.

The ground hums. The lights around each of you begin to shimmer, uncertain, unstable. A choice has been made.

And the shackles start to loosen.

The Mirror wavers, momentarily shaken by Finn's defiance.

The Shackles still glow yet no longer invincible.

Finn lowers his hands, breath rough, his voice steadier now. "If I can speak... we *all* can."

That's when Thalia speaks. Their voice is soft, meanwhile they ring with purpose. **"We've been separated,"** they say. "By the belief that our strength only matters in isolation." They look around at the glowing cells, their eyes sharp with understanding. **"We were never meant to break this alone."**

Inside their pillar of light, they press both palms to the edges. The energy flickers at their touch, responding to *intention*.

Kael, still grounded in his clarity, closes his eyes as light begins to gather around his form. **"These Shackles thrive in silence,"** he says. "In the silence of disconnection. Of forgetting we were always stronger together." He places a hand over his heart, the light around him pulsing in rhythm with his breath. **"Let's speak to each other with our will."**

Thalia nods, then reaches one hand toward Kael, even through the barrier. As if answering an unseen current, Kael mirrors the gesture.

For a moment—nothing.

Then, softly, their two veils of light begin to stretch—threads of silver and white reaching toward one another, trembling, testing.

And then—touch.

Where their light connects, a pulse of energy flares. The two separate cells ripple—and begin to merge. Their lights fuse as a *synthesis*.

Unity.

They turn—now standing within one larger pillar—toward Ardyn, who crouches inside his own veil, eyes shadowed, fists limp against the glowing surface.

He looks... small. Smaller than you've ever seen him.

Silent.

The Mirror's words still echo in his cell.

"You always go too far."

"No one wants you around."

"You're too much."

"You ruin things."

Thalia calls gently, "Ardyn—come back. We need your fire. You *are* fire."

Kael extends his hand toward him, voice steady. **"Even the brightest flame dims in silence; Yours was never meant to burn alone."**

Ardyn looks up slowly—pain etched across his face like heat cracks in stone. But something in his eyes... *lands*. His fists tighten. He pushes against the veil with breath and **willingness.** The cell quivers and the light from Kael and Thalia's joined veil extends outward and **pulls him in.**

The moment Ardyn steps into their light, his head bows in surrender.

To trust.

To connection.

And then—Finn's light reaches them. The strength of his truth, still glowing like a hearth, draws toward Ardyn's fire. Their cells **meld**—brightening.

Now four stand in one.

Zara watches from across the divide, hands trembling, her own veil still untouched.

The Mirror speaks:

"They never really saw you."

"You were just a tool. A convenience."

"No one stays."

Zara closes her eyes. A single tear rolls down her cheek. She lifts her chin, whispering to herself. **"I stayed. When others left, I stayed. And now... I choose to be seen."** The light around her cracks, shimmers and then stretches, drawn by the warmth of the group already united.

Zara steps forward. Her cell collapses behind her, merging with theirs.

One light.

Five voices.

One rhythm.

Then—

Eric's hand slams against the edge of his veil, grinning fiercely. "I don't need to be asked twice."

Celeste smiles softly. "I saw this before it happened."

Their lights extend— two currents of clarity and confidence and as they touch, their veils fold inward, linking to the main cell like stars falling into constellation.

Seven now.

And only one remains apart.

You.

Your cell stands slightly distant, just farther.

And the crew turns toward you, each of them, nonetheless inviting.

Kael steps forward, placing a hand over his heart. **"We're here. You've held space for all of us. Let us hold it for you now."**

Zara nods. "This part is yours."

Thalia's voice comes next. "It's time."

Eric smiles, his eyes bright. "Use what you know."

Celeste raises her hand toward you with trust. "You don't have to say it out loud," she says softly. "Just remember who you are."

Journal Prompt III: Unbinding the Voice

Take a breath. Let it travel all the way down to the depths of your being.

This space is for you. When you're ready, let these questions gently invite something deeper forward:

1. What truth have I always known, but have stayed silent about because someone once convinced me it wouldn't matter?
   (And what happens when I allow that truth to rise now?)

2. Whose words have I carried for too long—words that were never mine, but shaped me anyway?
   (And what would my voice sound like if I finally let them go?)

3. If I no longer had to protect myself from being "too much" or "not enough"..., who would I finally allow myself to become?

These are not questions to answer with the mind alone. They're invitations to remember. To reclaim. To rise. Your silence once protected you. Now your voice will *set you free.*

You remember in *essence.* A truth that rose when all others fell away.

And then it happens.

The light around you shifts from *alignment.*

The moment your truth stirs, your veil begins to ripple—thread by thread, stretching toward the unified light of the crew.

When it touches theirs, there is no sound. Only a pulse.

A breath.

A *joining.*

And in that instant, **the Shackles break.**

The veils collapse—not into emptiness but into a singular, glowing field of shared strength. Eight lights become one.

The Mirror of Shadows trembles. Its face reforms—mouth wide, featureless, desperate to speak. The words no longer land. They bounce back, hollow. Directionless.

"You... don't deserve..."

The mouth opens again. But nothing comes out.

Only   static.

Only silence.

Cracks begin to form across its surface. Small at first. Then spreading like fractures in glass too long under pressure.

Eric steps forward, his voice steady as stone. "People who are loud and wrong only feel powerful when they can project their pain into someone else's silence."

Kael nods beside him, soft light coiling around his palms. "And yet when silence is healed," he says, "it becomes a mirror that shows them who they truly are—empty of truth. Full of noise."

The Mirror falters.

And the voice is gone.

Only the sound of breath remains. Eight souls, one circle, standing in quiet defiance.

Then—

Ardyn turns to you. His eyes burn with pride. "Seeker," he says, voice low. "Look at your weapon."

And so you do. You notice that it glows with **clarity**. It pulses with every truth you've chosen. Every false name you've released. Every step you've taken back toward yourself.

Celeste steps forward, her hand resting over her chest. "This is the moment," she says, "when you stop searching. And start *becoming*." She meets your gaze. "Cast it. Into the veil."

You lift your weapon.

It isn't heavy.

It's *familiar*.

Like something you've always carried and finally, you know how to wield.

You close your eyes to remember.

I release what no longer defines me. I reclaim my voice. My vision. My vibration.

The weapon hums with that knowing.

You open your eyes.

And let it fly.

It cuts through the air like a vow made visible.

It strikes the veil.

And the world shatters.

Light erupts—not violent, but *pure*.

The Shackles dissolve in an instant.

The Mirror explodes inward, its twisted reflections curling into dust like lies exposed to truth.

Silence follows.

The stone behind the mirror's glass groans—then splits, the final remnants of resistance crumbling to the ground in reverent defeat.

The cavern opens.

Wide. Ancient. Waiting.

From within, air flows outward and *aware*.

There is something in the dark.

It doesn't threaten.

It *listens*.

The Moyux is waiting.

Kael steps beside you. "You've done what few ever dared," he says. "You've faced yourself and reclaimed your voice."

Eric nods, pride written across his features. "And now," he adds, "you don't speak with words—you speak with *truth*."

Celeste gazes toward the opening, her voice quiet. "You've shattered the voices that once defined you." She turns to you. "Now, you walk forward not to seek yourself— "But to *meet* the truth that's been waiting for you all along."

CHAPTER 8:

WHISPERS FROM THE CHILD WITHIN

You step through the threshold and something shifts. Not in the grey solid stone, and not in the silence of the air.

But inside of *you*.

The Realm no longer resists your presence. It *receives* you.

The echoes are gone. The projections have faded. This is not a place for testing. This is a place for remembering.

The crew remains behind, gathered just beyond the mouth of the cavern because they understand: This next part of the journey is yours alone.

They do not speak. They bear witness. Still and reverent, holding the space while you step deeper into yourself.

You begin to walk. The floor beneath your boots is smoother here as though worn down by time, or memory. The farther you go, the quieter it becomes.

No voices. No pulsing light. Just the sound of your breath and the soft, almost imperceptible rhythm of your heartbeat—reminding you: *you are still here.*

You pass through a narrow passage where the air grows warmer. Softer. Like stepping into something sacred.

And then—

You arrive.

A small chamber, round and still. No light, yet nothing is dark. The space glows faintly from within itself, like breath illuminating bone. In the center of the chamber is a pool. The water is clear. Still. Reflective. Unlike the mirrors you've faced before, this reflection holds no distortion.

No voices.

No challenge.

It simply waits.

And beside the pool—

You see them.

A child.

They sit quietly, cross-legged, their toes just brushing the water's edge.

Their hands rest in their lap.

Their clothes are simple. Familiar.

And their eyes—

Their eyes are yours.

Not who you are now.

Who you once were.

Before the shaping.

Before the silence.

Before you learned to question your own light.

They see you.

And in that seeing, you feel your shoulders soften. You hadn't realized how tightly you'd been holding yourself together. You take a step closer. The stone beneath your feet is cool and smooth. Your weapon, at your side, hums faintly with *awareness*.

The child doesn't flinch.

They do not speak. The moment your gaze meets theirs, you hear something within: *"Will you sit with me?"*

You look back at the crew as they follow behind you in silence. Kael looks at you and nods. Eric places his right hand on your shoulder and gives you the look of confidence.

And so, you walk towards the child. And you begin to sit with them.

Perhaps not by choice, but by gravity.

You lower yourself slowly, carefully.

The stone is grounding.

The silence is full.

They do not ask for your story. They do not ask what you've become. They only want to know: *"Do you remember?"* And even if you don't yet have words... something in you begins to answer.

You sit beside the child. There is no urgency. No task. Just the quiet rhythm of their breath syncing with your own—slow, even, steady.

They reach into the water with small fingers and swirl it gently. No ripples reach you. Only memory. And suddenly, without being shown, you begin to remember.

A moment.

Then another.

Some are soft.

Others ache.

You see your younger self turning away after being told you were too much.

You hear laughter that wasn't kind.

You feel the quiet where praise should have been.

And the pause... where someone could have said they were proud of you, instead they didn't.

The child watches you with compassion. They are not asking for you to fix what happened.

Only to *feel it.* With them.

And as the memories rise, something else does too.

A truth.

You were never too much. You were never not enough.

You were sensitive because you felt the world deeply.

You were quiet because your thoughts were rich.

You were loud because your joy didn't know how to be contained.

You didn't break. You adapted.

The child leans slightly toward you. Their expression is gentle, still curious. You may not have answers. But you have something even more important: presence. They place their hand gently on your knee. And though they say nothing, you know what they're asking: *"Will you stay?"*

You don't need to speak. Your breath, slow and grounded, says yes. You feel your chest soften. Your shoulders lower. Your grip on everything you thought you had to hold loosens.

"I see you now, thank you. And I'm not leaving." And in that moment, they smile with relief. Slowly, they rise to their feet. And reach out. Their hand presses lightly over your heart, and you feel it:

A warmth. A glow from *within.* The child is not returning to you. They never left. They were just waiting for you to remember how to listen. Their form begins to shimmer, dissolve and merge. The glow wraps gently around your ribcage. Settles into your hands. Your spine and your breath. And as they fade fully into you, you feel yourself grow whole.

Behind you, the weapon at your side flickers once with soft golden light. The pulse of a memory is integrated.

The mission it carries is no longer distant.

It's personal.

Ahead, the cavern narrows into a dark corridor.

The air has changed.

Journal Prompt I

Place one hand over your heart and the other just below your ribs. Feel the breath move between them. Let this be a moment of presence, of reunion.

Your Inner Child is not a stranger. They are a part of you who once held everything you couldn't. And perhaps... they still do.

Now, gently ask:

1. What part of me learned to hide—staying small, staying silent—to feel safe in a world that didn't always feel safe to be seen? *Whose love, judgment, or rules shaped that choice? And what part of me still carries that habit today?*

2. When I imagine sitting beside the child I once were... what do I notice in their eyes? *What emotion do they carry? How do they respond to my presence?*

3. What do they still believe about me and what truth do I now carry that they need to hear? *Speak to them gently. What wisdom have you gathered that could bring them peace?*

4. If love, safety, and belonging were already mine...

   » How would my Inner Child move?

   » What would they ask for?

   » What would they finally allow themselves to feel?

These are not questions to be solved. They are invitations. Let the answers come as words, images, sensations... Or silence. Because sometimes, being *present* is more healing than being right.

The Agents That Split

Eric and the others rush over to your side.

Celeste speaks first. "That was such a beautiful moment with your inner child. Real transformation takes place once we remember the innocence we lost in place of the pain we gathered along the way."

Ardyn and Finn are both teary eyes.

Ardyn then says, "You were such a cute little spark, I nearly melted from the sweetness in you."

The chamber of the Inner Child fades behind you but something new emerges from within. Your breath moves differently now. Steadier. Deeper. Like you're no longer just moving forward, but returning. The path ahead curves downward into a long, torchless corridor. The walls shimmer faintly with *echoes.*

You don't hear your footsteps. You hear... voices.

Familiar.

Terribly familiar.

"You had to be strong, so I learned how to fight."

"You were ashamed, so I learned how to disappear."

"You were scared, so I stayed angry—for both of us."

They don't come from ahead.

They come from *within the walls.*

And then—slowly—figures begin to emerge.

Not monsters.

Not illusions.

Agents.

Each one carries a version of your face, warped by the role they were forced to play:

Agent Anger

Clad in cracked obsidian armor, jaw clenched, fists burning with slow embers. His eyes are sharp and calculating. He paces like someone who's guarded your gates too long.

"I stood between you and everything," he growls. "Hurt me, not them. That was the deal." His voice is fire yet beneath it, a tremble of fatigue.

Agent Guilt

Thin. Hollow-eyed. Draped in robes stitched with fragments of broken promises and replayed memories. She holds a ledger in one hand. It glows with tally marks. Each one... yours.

"I kept score," she says quietly. "I made sure you never forgot who you failed."

There's no malice in her. Only sorrow that calcified into identity.

Agent Silence

He stands behind the others, nearly invisible. Pale and still, wrapped in the shadows between your words. Not cloaked—but *absent.* His voice is barely audible.

"They said it was easier when you didn't speak. So I stopped."

Celeste steps beside you, her blades lowered. Her voice calm.

"These aren't enemies," she murmurs. "They're echoes that forgot they were echoes."

Kael narrows his eyes, watching them with a healer's intuition.

"They once served your survival. However now... they serve something else."

He gestures toward the far end of the corridor.

A deep, pulsing shadow flickers there. Not fully formed yet *watching.*

The Moyux.

Not here yet, nonetheless present.

You grip your weapon to anchor it in. It vibrates faintly in your hand, as if it senses something sacred is near.

Eric's voice comes from behind, quiet and firm: "They can't touch you. Not unless you believe what they say."

Ardyn scoffs and cracks his knuckles, fire blooming briefly in his palm. Then he exhales, and lets the flame fade. "We could fight them," he says. "However that's not what they need. Nor what *you* need."

Thalia's voice floats in from your other side. "Ask them why they stayed so long. Then ask yourself why you let them."

The agents stand motionless now. Waiting to be *acknowledged.*

This is not a battle.

This is the turning point.

The reconciliation of everything you once became to survive.

Reconciliation

You step forward. Not in defiance but in recognition.

Agent Anger raises his head at your approach. The fire in his fists dims, yet it does not vanish.

He stands tall, shoulders squared, armor cracked from too many battles fought without rest. He doesn't speak first. Because he's waiting to see if you're here to fight him.

Or finally *see* him.

You say nothing however your body answers. You lower your weapon to show you've come with truth, not war. And with that, he exhales. A breath of exhaustion.

"Do you remember the first time I rose for you?" he asks.

Memory flickers.

The moment someone raised their voice at you and you clenched your fists, even though you were shaking.

You didn't know how to respond, yet something inside you roared: *"Never again."*

"You didn't have the words back then, so I became them," he continues. He takes a step closer, the heat from his form radiating outward. "I took every blow. Bit my tongue until it bled. Snapped before anyone else could." He pauses. And then his voice shifts *clearer.* "Despite this, you never asked me to stop. Not once."

A silence grows between you.

Not shame.

Reflection.

He gestures to the cracks in his armor.

"I broke things I wanted to protect. Burned bridges that could have held. Not because I hated you but because I didn't know how to let anyone else in."

You feel it now.

The fire was never your enemy.

It was your shield.

Your scream.

Your promise to never be hurt again.

And it kept that promise... at a cost.

He waits to be *acknowledged.*

Zara's voice echoes gently from behind. "Anger only becomes the enemy when it forgets who it was meant to protect."

Kael places his hands on your shoulders and speaks to offer words of wisdom before you take action: *"Remember Seeker, when the masks fall, and the shadows soften, what remains is who you've chosen to become."*

And so, you breathe.

And you begin to wonder...

Ritual Reflection: The Fire That Served

1. When was the first time I had to get loud just to feel heard? And beneath the roar... what was I really longing for? *(Safety? Respect? A space to just be?)*

2. In what ways did anger give me strength, especially when I didn't yet know how to ask for help? Think of a time it rose up to set a boundary that your words couldn't.

3. What might shift right now if I stopped treating anger as the enemy and began listening to it as a protector? What does it want me to notice? What might it be asking me to reclaim?

These are not confessions. They are recognitions. The fire was never your enemy. It only wanted to be seen as *loyalty*.

The agent kneels in surrender. He places a gauntleted hand over his chest, where a faint glow pulses beneath the armor— the ember of a younger wound.

"If you no longer need me to rage..." he says quietly, "then teach me how to protect you... without burning everything down."

And with that, he opens his hand. In his palm, a glowing coal. It hovers softly, weightless, warm.

A gift. The power to protect with clarity.

You reach forward. Your hand closes around it. It doesn't burn. It glows.

And Agent Anger dissolves into light, *returning to* you.

Behind you, the crew remains still. Watching yet *honoring*.

And before you know, the next figure steps forward.

The one with tally marks carved into their robe. The one who held every "what if" like a wound that never closed.

The coal still glows in your hand, just warm. Alive. Anchored. Yours.

Agent Guilt.

She walks slowly. Carefully. As though every step carries the weight of a thousand "should've and could've."

In her arms, she carries a ledger, massive, swollen, spine fraying from too many pages jammed into its seams. Loose sheets stick out at odd angles, some yellowed with age, others smeared with ink that never fully dried. She clutches it like something sacred. Like something painful. When she lifts her gaze, there is no accusation. Only weariness.

She stops in front of you and opens the ledger with trembling hands. Pages flutter by memory. One stops. She reads:

"I should have seen it coming."

"I should have done more."

"I should have known better."

Her voice doesn't cut. It confesses.

She doesn't look at you—yet.

"You didn't ask me with words," she murmurs. "Every time you whispered, 'I failed them,' or 'It was my fault'..., you hired me." Her thumb traces a torn edge in the paper. "I stayed because guilt felt like growth. Like penance. Like proof that you still cared."

She swallows. "Over time, I forgot what I was guarding. I started guarding the pain itself." She lifts the ledger, slowly, reverently. To show you. To ask if you still want her to carry it.

Kael steps beside you now, voice like gentle stone. "Some wounds repeat until they're released."

Thalia speaks from the other side, hand over their heart. "Guilt can't teach the lesson if you keep punishing the student."

You look at Agent Guilt. Her arms shake from the weight. Her eyes soft, tired, honest, waiting for your permission. You don't take the ledger. You take her hand. And for a moment, the weight she's carried becomes shared.

Then seen.

Then set down.

Ritual Reflection: Forgiving the Ledger

1. What internal rule, written by guilt, have I lived by that no longer serves who I'm becoming?
   And whose voice did that rule *really* belong to? *(A parent? A teacher? A past version of me?)*

2. What part of me once believed guilt was the only path to being responsible or good?
   And if I released self-punishment... what would growth look like instead?

3. If I could thank guilt for what it tried to teach me, without needing to carry its weight...

What wisdom would I choose to keep? What would I gently lay down, here and now?

Agent Guilt exhales. A slow, deep breath, like someone breathing for the first time. She tears a single page from the old ledger.

One line.

One memory.

And places it in your open hand.

You read it slowly with recognition.

"Carrying the weight felt safer than setting it down."

And somehow, you understand.

It was never about punishment.

It was about protection.

Preservation.

Survival.

You close your hand around the page and it dissolves in light.

You have the feeling of it not being erased. The calming sensation of it finally being *Released from guilt and Reclaimed with understanding.*

The warmth lingers in your palm from the truth it no longer needs to carry.

The air shifts.

And you feel him before you see him.

Agent Silence.

He doesn't emerge. He simply is, as though he's been standing there the entire time, just outside your field of awareness.

He's wrapped in faded muted tones and colorless fabric of forgetting. His presence doesn't announce itself. It retreats even as it arrives. His face is familiar, yet undefined—soft around the edges, like a memory you were never supposed to revisit. He doesn't meet your gaze. Doesn't speak. And that, somehow, is the loudest thing of all. He stands still. Head bowed. Hands clasped tightly in front of him, holding something you can't yet see.

You recognize the stance. It's yours. The version of you that learned early:

If I stay quiet, I stay safe.

If I don't speak, I won't be wrong.

If I disappear, they won't leave me.

Celeste's voice rises gently behind you, like wind through trees. "This one doesn't protect you from danger. He protects you from being seen."

Zara adds softly, hand over her heart. "He made silence feel like sanctuary... until it became a cage."

You step closer. He flinches from the habit of shrinking. And then, with a voice barely more than a breath, he speaks.

"I didn't want to be a burden." He swallows. **"So I stayed quiet. And over time... I forgot how to speak."**

He looks up. And you see it—the eyes that once shone with wonder, now dimmed with decades of unspoken words.

He opens his hands and what was invisible before becomes clear: **Thread.**

Thin, silken strands unravel from his fingers, each one tied to a moment you chose silence over truth.

Some are tangled.

Some frayed.

Some pulled so tight they still leave marks you forgot you carried.

He lets the threads fall.

They do not snap.

They simply... loosen.

Ritual Reflection:
The Power of Unspoken Words

1. What truth have I kept hidden, not because I didn't know it, but because I feared it wouldn't be received with care?
What did I imagine would happen if I spoke it aloud?

2. When did silence first feel like safety?
And at what point did that silence begin to feel like invisibility?

3. If I could whisper one thing to the part of me that stayed quiet for so long...
What would I want them to feel? What do they deserve to hear now?

Agent Silence steps closer to be witnessed.

You don't offer words. You offer presence.

You place your hand gently over your throat and feel something warm pulse beneath your skin.

A promise.

He watches.

And smiles.

It is faint. But real.

Then he dissolves. Into stillness.

And from that stillness, you rise.

The silence is expectant.

The ground hums faintly beneath your feet, a resonance, as though the Realm itself is listening for what you'll say next.

Somewhere deeper within, the Moyux stirs, ready to receive you.

The Fall Beneath Knowing

It begins with stillness.

Too still.

The kind of stillness that doesn't belong to silence, but to anticipation.

The chamber vibrates softly beneath your feet.

A hum.

A whisper.

A warning.

Then—

A voice.

It doesn't shout. It doesn't echo. It curls like smoke through your ribs.

"So close... and still you believe this ends with light."

Before anyone can answer, the ground fractures deliberately. Like something ancient unfolding a truth it can no longer keep hidden.

Cracks form a perfect circle beneath your group.

Finn's stance widens.

Zara draws breath—too late.

The floor gives way.

And you fall.

There is no scream.

Only descent.

The world above narrows into a slit of memory, then vanishes.

You fall past walls that never end, through darkness that doesn't feel empty—it feels watchful.

Your crew spirals with you, suspended, drifting as though caught in a sea of mirrored breath.

The deeper you fall, the thicker the air becomes until it isn't air at all. It's reflection.

Liquid silver.

Pooled memory.

You fall through fragments of yourself—moments you never thought would find you again:

Your childlike laughter, distant and unguarded.

A look of betrayal you never allowed to surface.

A door you closed.

A truth you buried.

A love you abandoned.

Each image floats past as if deciding whether to follow you down.

And then, you stop. Not with impact. But with arrival.

You land on something smooth and lightless. A floor that doesn't reflect light—only *intention*.

The others follow, feet touching ground soundlessly, forming a circle around you.

Kael steadies himself.

Celeste's blades glow faintly—then dim. Even steel respects this place.

The world around you unfurls.

You are standing in a space made entirely of mirrors, but none of them face outward.

They face in.

They do not reflect your body.

They reflect your fears.

Your fragments.

Your unchosen selves.

And from the center of the space.Not walking, not crawling— yet emerging—comes a figure.

Shifting.

Unfinished.

Too many shapes wrapped into one.

The space folds around *accepting*.

Because this is its domain.

CHAPTER 9:
THE ONE YOU TRIED TO BURY

The cavern pulses.

It's not light that moves—it's something heavier. More ancient. Presence.

The air tightens around your lungs like hands that remember your name. The space feels deeper than it looks. Wider than it should be. A stillness that doesn't welcome—it waits.

Then a sound tears through it.

Not a roar. Not a whisper.

A fractured wind, like breath dragged across broken stone.

The crew tenses.

And from the darkness, it steps forward.

The Moyux.

It doesn't charge. It doesn't scream. It simply arrives—slow as dusk—and somehow older than fear itself. Its form doesn't shimmer or shift in dramatic spectacle. No. It flickers more subtly, like memory made flesh. Truths you never wanted to speak... given skin.

119

At first, it wears the face of a stranger. Then someone you once loved. Then someone who betrayed you.

Then—

Your own.

It stands in silence, letting the familiarity do its work.

And then, the voice. Not out loud but inside you. Around you. A vibration in the ribs.

"You made it further than I thought. But not without me."

The Moyux walks slowly, its form like liquid shadow, each step dragging some long-lost emotion back into view. Beneath its surface: too many eyes. Too many mouths. All of them saying things you once believed.

"I've been here since the beginning. Feeding on every apology you didn't owe. Every smile you used to keep the peace. Every night you said, 'I'm fine,' while quietly unraveling."

It smiles. Not cruelly. Not kindly. Something in between. Something that says *I know you better than they ever could.*

"I kept you safe when silence was all you had. I stepped in each time you said yes because you feared what would happen if you didn't." The temperature shifts. You feel the crew begin to move.

Ardyn's fists flare with heat, his jaw clenched tight.

Thalia glances at you, already calculating defense.

Finn's grip tightens around his weapon.

Eric's hand is held in the air, with the signal to hold steady and his face is fierce while sparks of fire and lightning surround him.

Kael's staff is positioned ready to strike with his sigils glowing violently. Celeste and Zara are also at the ready in a position to support in any way they can.

They know. This thing can hurt them.

But not you.

"You thought healing meant leaving me behind. But all you've done is gather the pieces I was made of. I am who you became...

when control was the only way to feel safe. Why resist me now?" The voice weaves into your chest—knowing. "You've outgrown them, haven't you? Their hopes. Their fears. You don't need to be *understood* when you could finally be *obeyed*."

It turns to face your crew, gaze lingering like a blade hovering before a cut.

"They can't follow you where you're going. They see your journey, but I am your journey. I was there for every apology you didn't owe. Every moment you wanted to scream but smiled instead. Every time you made yourself smaller just to be loved."

Its gaze returns to you. Eyes like obsidian, reflecting every fractured moment you thought you had buried. And something tightens in your gut. You can't deny.

"Only I know what you're becoming," it says.

Silence.

Then a step forward from Eric. He moves like the ground beneath him belongs to him. His boots steady, his coat settling around him like armor he doesn't need. The usual glint in his eyes is gone. What remains is conviction.

"That's enough," Eric says. "You don't get to rewrite their story just because you were part of the prologue."

He doesn't raise a weapon. His presence is enough. "They chose to come here. Chose to look. Chose to feel. That wasn't *you*. That was *them*. And you're not here because they're weak. You're here because they're ready."

The Moyux tilts its head, amused. "Ah... the Igniter," it murmurs. "So loyal. So certain." A smile curls like smoke. "Tell me, then—where were you when they wept in silence? When *my* voice was the only one that stayed?" Then it turns to you. "I'm not your enemy. I'm the version of you that survived when you couldn't afford to fall apart."

Eric falters. His mouth opens but no words come.

121

Then Zara answers. She steps forward, illusion magic curling around her fingers as memory. "We all have shadows," she says gently. "But they walked through theirs."

She raises her palm, and a shimmer pulses into the air above it—a vivid mirage of your journey:

Your silhouette emerging from the fog.

Your hands trembling but lifted.

The moment your weapon took shape, forged from purpose.

"You didn't bring them here," Zara continues. "You just survived the parts they abandoned. That's not power. That's pain with no place to go."

The Moyux's form ripples, growing less defined.

It no longer smiles.

"So be it," it hisses. The voice drops—gravel scraping stone.

Something ancient awakens in the floor. The vibrations rise *through* you. The ground becomes fluid. Stone folds inward like a closing throat.

The crew shouts but the sound is swallowed inward.

The trial has begun.

The Breaking Point

The ground doesn't shake. It *remembers*.

A low hum rises from beneath your feet but something more ancient. Like the cavern is exhaling after holding its breath for centuries.

And you feel it in your bones.

The vibrations crawl through your soles, your spine, your ribs until even your heartbeat feels like someone else's memory. The air thickens. Heavy. Electric with truths you haven't yet spoken.

Then—

Fire.

Ardyn moves like a drawn blade. His body taut, voice sharp enough to split stone. Flames curl around his fists. This isn't rage. It's *alignment.*

"I've watched them earn every scar," he growls, fire licking the edges of his coat. "You don't get to twist that into some kind of return."

He thrusts his arms forward, and a burst of fire tears through the space between you and the Moyux—gold, clean, crackling with intent.

It strikes.

But the Moyux doesn't burn.

The flame passes through it like breath through fog—dissolving, unraveling, *changing.*

The fire becomes vapor. The vapor becomes shimmer. The shimmer becomes memory.

The Moyux responds, "You think I'm trying to stop them? I'm trying to bring them home. Back to what made them strong when no one else knew how."

And suddenly—

It rains moments of the past.

A quiet room you never escaped.

A chair you sat in for too long.

A hand you almost reached for but didn't.

A goodbye you rehearsed but never gave.

The memories don't strike like lightning.

They *seep.*

Soft. Sticky. Real.

Your chest tightens.

Your knees lock.

You feel the old ache behind your eyes, like the edge of a cry you refused to have.

Around you, your crew falters.

Zara staggers back, her illusion magic glitching into half-formed shapes—her own face, her childhood smile, a desert sky long gone.

Kael lets out a strangled breath, pressing one hand to his chest as if to steady a heart that's seen too much truth at once.

Finn's shoulders lift in instinct by his strength rising to hold the memory of what couldn't be held back then.

"You dressed your survival in poetry," the Moyux murmurs, voice velvet-wrapped steel. "But I was there—in every verse. The silence you made sacred. The numbness you named healing."

Its presence expands—without movement. Just *knowing*.

And then...

A rumble beneath the stone. A sigh of fate.

You don't see the mirrors rise. You feel them.

The ground tilts—subtly, like a dream shifting.

And then—

They appear.

Tall. Flawless. Soundless.

Like they were always meant to be here.

Like the room has finally remembered its purpose.

The mirrors rise—tall as obelisks, silent as stone.

They encircle you. Seven in total.

Each one hums with familiar magic, yet none feel like safety. They feel... inevitable. Like altars built for forgetting.

The Moyux doesn't gloat. It simply lifts a hand.

And the first is taken.

Zara.

She's mid-spell, threads of illusion coiling from her fingertips. Her eyes widen with realization.

"No—"

The word vanishes with her as the mirror closes, sealing her inside.

A glimmer of desert wind remains, then fades.

Her reflection doesn't plead.

It waits.

Finn tries to brace, planting his feet in grounding stance. His eyes never leave you.

"I can hold—"

But the mirror envelops him.

You see his hand press to the glass—gently.

Celeste steps forward, one hand already outstretched, trying to track the shifting paths.

"This was always a test of alignment," she mouths.

Then the mirror claims her, folding light around her like a frozen horizon.

Her reflection doesn't panic.

It studies.

Always navigating.

Kael falters. His breath catches, his body shimmering briefly with healing sigils.

But no spell comes.

The mirror wraps him in quiet.

A soft blue glow flickers once—then goes still.

Thalia's voice echoes.

"Keep going."

Their hand lifts in silent encouragement, then disappears behind a veil of radiant glass.

Ardyn resists.

His flames surge in defiance, golden light pulsing from his chest.

"I'll burn through this!"

But the mirror doesn't fight him.

It waits.

And when he exhausts the blaze, it takes him, silently.

His reflection remains a spark behind the glass, still burning.

And then—

Eric.

He hasn't moved.

He watches each mirror seal—his jaw tight, hands still at his sides.

You expect him to fight.

He doesn't.

He looks at you.

And smiles.

Softly.

"You started this journey with a book in your hand," he says. "But you're the one who carried it all this way."

He closes his eyes and lets the mirror take him.

No resistance.

No fear.

Just trust.

The curtain draws shut on a chapter he knew would end. Not in goodbye but in becoming.

And now—

You are alone.

The mirrors shimmer around you.

The Moyux steps forward, but it does not attack. It gestures.

And the cavern begins to shift.

The air folds inward.

The stone beneath your feet softens—then hardens again, in new shape.

Walls stretch higher. Vines of shadow curl into arches.

The ceiling gives way to a high dome, moonlight pouring through a single open circle.

And at the center—floating, waiting—

The Mirror of Sovereignty.

Surrounded by four broken columns.

Surrounded by memory.

And behind it all—

The Moyux.

The Moyux turns toward you.

It does not threaten.

It *offers.*

"Come closer, and let me show you... the future that could be yours," it whispers.

The Mirror Speaks

The chamber hums with a silence too full to be called empty.

Overhead, the beam of light pouring through the temple's circular opening casts soft illumination across the room. The alabaster stone glows with something more than reflection—something living. The vines along the walls gently stir, as if sensing the shift in you.

At the center, suspended above a shallow pool of still water, floats the Mirror of Sovereignty.

It waits.

You approach—not out of conquest, but completion.

Behind you, the broken columns lean like guardians of forgotten truths, each one cracked but still standing. The room feels like breath held in the space between recognition and revelation.

The Moyux steps forward beside you but as something that once had power over you but no longer does.

Its voice, when it speaks, is hushed. Steady.

"You've come far. Further than I imagined. But you didn't get here by banishing your shadows. You invited them in."

It gestures to the Mirror.

"Let it show you who you carry now."

The Mirror ripples—like a pulse. Then clarifies.

And in its surface, you see them.

Agent Anger stands first—his fire dimmed but not extinguished. His arms are crossed, his expression proud. Not in dominance, but devotion. He nods once, a silent vow of protection that no longer demands destruction. "I no longer burn to be heard," his reflection says. "I burn to light the way."

Beside him, **Agent Guilt** turns another page in her heavy ledger. But this time, her hands are steady. She no longer writes—she reflects. She looks up and meets your gaze through the mirror. "I carried the weight so you wouldn't forget," she whispers. "But you've remembered. I can rest now."

Then, **Agent Silence**. They no longer hide behind a veil. Their mouth doesn't move—but their eyes speak volumes. There is music in their stillness. A quiet power that no longer fears being misunderstood. "I kept your truth safe," they murmur inside your mind. "Now, it's safe with you."

You feel it—not just recognition, but *reintegration.*

These aren't just echoes. They are you as *wisdom.*

The mirror holds the moment. Its light intensifies slightly—then softens.

And slowly...

Their reflections fade as completion.

Only the surface of the Mirror remains now—smooth, waiting.

The Moyux watches with quiet reverence.

"They've returned to you," it says. "And so have you to yourself."

Then, almost wistfully: "I wonder... are you ready for the final one?"

From behind the glass, a figure steps forward.

Graceful.

Polished.

The Performer.

They wear your face, but a version refined into something curated. Their movements are fluid, poised. A thousand small adjustments—posture, smile, glance—each one designed to be liked, to be praised, to never cause discomfort.

They are elegant. And exhausting.

In one hand, they carry a bouquet of masks—each sculpted from some past performance.

The Good Listener.

The Overachiever.

The Strong One.

The One Who Never Needed Help.

The One Who Was Always Okay.

The Performer stops just inside the mirror's edge. They do not speak at first. Their eyes search yours with an ache so old, it almost feels sacred.

Then, softly: "We made it this far," they say. I helped get us here."

Their voice is yours—gentler, maybe. The voice you used when you were trying not to cry. The voice that told others, "Don't worry about me."

"They loved us," they continue. "Not because of who we were... but who we became for them."

They lift one of the masks. A smile carved into porcelain. "I wore this one the longest."

The Moyux watches, silent now—its role, no longer dominant, has become that of a witness.

You step forward, closer to the Mirror. Closer to the part of you that survived... by performing.

The Performer's eyes flicker. They set the mask down slowly. "I wasn't lying," they whisper. "I just thought being lovable meant being less." They look down. "You started showing parts of yourself

I didn't understand. Parts that weren't perfect. Weren't pleasing. And they stayed. The crew stayed. You stayed."

They breathe—a tremor in their perfect composure.

"Maybe you don't need me anymore."

The Moyux finally speaks softly with respect. "They were your protector," it says. "The last one. The final threshold between performance... and presence." It nods toward the Mirror. "If you're ready, this is where the Performer returns—to rest."

You step closer.

The Performer meets your gaze—this time, with no pretense. No pose.

"Say something," they whisper. "Free me."

The Mirror glows gently.

It's time.

Final Reflection: The Sovereign Self

"When the masks fall, and the shadows soften,
what remains is who you've chosen to become."
—Kael

Answer the following prompts to complete your journey through the Realms of Reflection:

1. Which versions of myself did I once perform... just to feel safe, loved, or accepted?
   (And how did those roles help me survive?)

2. What parts of me were never broken, only buried?
   (How can I honor their return?)

3. What do I now choose to value, above all else, as I move forward in Sovereignty?
   (List four core values that feel alive in your body—not just ideas, but truths you're ready to live.)

4. If I could whisper one message to my future self during a moment of doubt, fear, or forgetting, what would I want them to remember about who we are now?

This closing ritual doesn't demand perfection. It offers something greater: **Ownership.**

You may now choose to walk forward to be enough…but as someone who already is.

The Integration

The Performer lowers their final mask—and gently lets it fall. It doesn't shatter. It simply dissolves into light. The Mirror's glow dims… then pulses again with choice.

The Moyux, still at the edge of the light, takes one slow step back. Its form begins to shift. Into something *softer.* Smaller. Human in a way you hadn't seen before. It drops to one knee before you. Its voice is quieter now. Not sinister. Just… honest. "I was made to protect you from what you weren't ready to feel. The shame. The grief. The rage. I swallowed it all so you could keep moving." It lifts its head and for the first time, there's no mask in its eyes. "But you're ready now. So if you'll have me… Let me become something new. *Within* you."

You don't need to speak. You just step forward. And as your hand touches its chest, there's no fear. Only remembrance. The weapon you forged—crafted from every truth, every wound, every realm you've crossed—responds. It glows in your hand with presence. You raise it to bless it.

The Moyux exhales, its whole form trembling like the last breath of a long-kept pain. And then, it dissolves.

Not in violence. In returning.

Radiant threads of light spiral inward, not outward.

Drawn back into your body. Into your chest.

Into the space it once protected.

And feared.

Integrated.

Reclaimed.

Remembered.

The Restoration

Silence holds the space like a closing prayer. Then—glass begins to melt and dissolve. The mirror prisons that once held your crew shimmer, soften, and release. One by one, they return.

Zara gasps as if surfacing from deep water. She clutches her chest, her eyes glistening from relief.

Finn says nothing. He doesn't need to. The look in his eyes is unmistakable: *You came back.*

Celeste appears next, blinking slowly, already reading the room like it's written in constellations. She nods to herself, as if this was always meant to be.

Thalia stumbles forward into Kael's arms. They hold each other for a breath longer than usual—then part without words, everything understood.

Ardyn's fire ignites across his hands in a brilliant flare but it doesn't burn. It celebrates. His grin is crooked, but proud.

And then, Eric. He steps through the final veil of light. There is something different in his eyes. Gratitude, yes. But also... awe. He walks straight to you and rests a firm, steady hand on your shoulder. "You did what none of us could. You faced what you were never meant to carry alone." His voice breaks slightly, but he holds it. "And you didn't destroy it. You transformed it."

Your gaze shifts toward the base of the temple.

Four columns surround the center where the Mirror once hovered.

Each one cracked, fractured, incomplete.

Still standing.

Still waiting.

Kael walks ahead, kneeling beside the nearest one, palm pressed to the stone.

"These were once your values," he says, his voice soft as prayer. "But they collapsed under the weight of silence, shame, and survival. Now... they can be rebuilt as you are."

Eric steps beside him and gestures toward your weapon. "Use what you made to consecrate."

Your hand tightens around the weapon you forged, etched with intention, memory, and meaning.

You walk toward the broken columns.

It hums faintly beneath your steps.

You raise your weapon and speak: "I reclaim what I once abandoned. I honor the strength that carried me through. This value is mine now because I choose it."

Light rises from the cracks.

The columns begin to restore—its foundation gleaming with new integrity.

Vines bloom. The walls breathe and above, a soft wind begins to circulate through the round opening in the ceiling.

Inside you.

Kael steps forward, placing his hand on your chest, not as a healer now, but as a witness.

"The Moyux was never your enemy," he says. "It was your exile. And you brought it home."

The temple glows brighter now. Six portals shimmer into view, opening one by one, each pulsing with the light of a different Realm.

Your next adventure awaits.

EPILOGUE:

THE CHOICE OF WHAT COMES NEXT

The temple is still, alive with a silence that listens.

Six portals shimmer in the space around you. They glow like invitations from distant stars, each pulsing with a truth you haven't yet lived… but somehow recognize.

You don't need directions.

Each one calls to a different part of your becoming.

Kael steps forward first. The portal before him swirls with flowing light and color—like breath, blood, and soul.

"This," he says, his voice deep and steady, "is the **Realm of Energy.** The realm where your vitality returns as presence. Where your body becomes a vessel for power, not pain. Where spirit and breath are no longer separate."He looks to the glowing blue arc above the portal and adds with quiet reverence: "If we go here, we'll begin in **Azurae**, the ancient homeland of the Jinn. A city of suspended bridges and luminous temples that stand in perfect balance between the physical and the spiritual. It is where I first learned to listen to both."

He steps back, and Zara glides forward—warmth rising in her smile as golden hues swirl within the second portal. "The **Realm of Abundance**," she says gently. "Not just wealth—but the freedom to receive. To allow. To know you are worthy of more without guilt." Her gaze lingers in the air. "We won't go to our homelands this time," she says. "We'll begin in the **Empire of Abubakari**—a kingdom once shaped by scarcity and now revered across the Realms. A living testament to what can be built when you stop defining yourself by what you lack."

Finn approaches next. His hand hovers near the third portal, which pulses in rose and crimson, like heartbeats made visible. "This is the **Realm of Love**," he says quietly. "Not just romance but *Relationship*. With others. With yourself. With the stories that shaped you." His brow furrows, but his tone is full of warmth. "We'll journey to the land of the **Jontel**, my people—where two tribes were torn apart by grief and pride. And still... they found their way back. Through forgiveness. Through family. Through *heart*."

He steps aside, and Ardyn strides forward, flame already crackling lightly at his palms. The fourth portal swirls with molten amber and sharp obsidian. "**The Realm of Mastery**," he says without hesitation. "Where we hone the craft of living.

Where excellence is forged not through ego, but through devotion to your deeper work."

He crosses his arms, nodding toward the swirling firelight. "We'll travel to the **Divided Lands** of the **Venasari and Soldari**, where my old mentor still carves wisdom into stone and strategy into warriors. There, skill is sacred. And your mastery... saves lives."

Thalia smiles softly as they glance toward Kael and Ardyn, then return to their place. But it's Celeste who moves next. She doesn't touch the portal before her. She simply faces it and the glow bends toward her like moonlight drawn to tide. The portal shows mountain peaks, distant drums, flickering candles, and hands passing gifts across generations.

"This is the **Realm of the Summit**," Celeste says. "Where past and future meet. Where you walk not just for yourself, but for those who came before... and those who will follow." Her voice lowers to a near-whisper. "We'll return to the sacred mountains of the **Venasari and Soldari** where I first heard the voice of legacy. Where service is not sacrifice... it is song."

The crew now forms a semicircle behind you, their words hanging in the air like woven cloth.

And then—Eric steps forward.

He doesn't say much at first. Just takes a long look at each portal. Then at you. "This is your moment," he says softly. "You faced your Moyux. You didn't run. You *remembered.* So now—this isn't a reward. It's a *return.* The Realms are offering you what was always yours: The power to choose."

He steps back.

Your weapon glows gently in your hand.

Just... ready.

Somewhere within, something rises.

A knowing.

Because the Realms were never just destinations.

They were mirrors.

And now—

You are no longer seeking. You are choosing.

As the six portals shimmer around you, each one a visible reflection of your healing path, another presence begins to form.

At first, it's just a shimmer in the far corner of the temple.

Subtle.

Half-hidden in shadow.

But Thalia turns toward it, already aware.

Eric follows, slower, gaze sharp. His expression shifts—not with fear, but with respect.

A seventh portal is forming.

Its glow is dimmer than the others—not dull, but veiled. Its light bends, masked in layers of violet and obsidian. You feel its vibration in your chest before you see it. It doesn't pulse like an invitation. It *beckons* like a secret.

"There's one more," Thalia says, stepping closer. "It doesn't announce itself like the others. It waits for those who need it most."

Eric stands beside them now, arms crossed, watching the portal ripple with shifting symbols and ancient glyphs. "This is the path to **Varne Roe**," he says quietly. "A realm of outlaws and pirates. Of broken codes and unspoken names." He glances at you. "There, the rule isn't to reveal—but to *protect.* It's where masks don't hide shame... they hold sovereignty."

Thalia steps closer, voice softer now. "In Varne Roe, the taboo becomes sacred. Pleasure, power, grief, desire—all the parts of yourself you were told not to feel...have a place." They trace a pattern in the air—half spell, half memory. "It's not safe in the way the others are. But it's honest. And honesty can heal the parts that couldn't find light anywhere else."

Eric rests a hand on the edge of the portal. "We don't have to go there now. But if you ever find a part of yourself that doesn't belong anywhere else..." He looks at you with something between invitation and warning. "You'll know where to go."

The seventh portal shimmers faintly.

Not louder.

Just *realer.*

The rest of the crew stands ready, facing the original six paths.

You stand at the threshold of every truth you've earned.

And somewhere within you, the knowing takes root:

You are no longer a Seeker lost in reflection—
You are a sovereign being, ready to choose.

APPENDIX

A Quick Guide to Understanding the Prompt Section

This book is not just meant to be read. It is meant to be felt. Woven throughout this journey are journal prompts designed to help you go beyond the words on the page and enter your own story. These prompts draw from practices in NLP (Neuro-Linguistic Programming), transformational coaching, and guided storytelling. They are invitations to reflect, feel, and remember who you are beneath the surface.

In my work as a guide, I have seen that true change comes when we stop analyzing and start embodying. We cannot just think our way into transformation. We must feel it in our bodies, experience it through our senses, and speak it back into our lives. That is why I use this method.

For those of us who carry layered identities and deep stories, it is easy to overthink and become disconnected from what we know in our bones. These questions are designed to help you come home to yourself. They are gentle tools to bypass the noise, access your inner wisdom, and reclaim your truth.

This process works because it brings together three powerful techniques:

Sensory-Based Access Questions

These ask you to recall what you saw, heard, or felt in a meaningful moment.

Why this matters: The body remembers what the mind forgets. When you access your senses, you return to a lived experience that reconnects you to your truth.

Personifying the Inner Voice

These prompts invite you to imagine your inner knowing speaking to you as a trusted guide, a friend, or a future version of yourself.

Why this matters: Sometimes clarity comes when we stop trying to solve and simply listen. Giving voice to your intuition helps you hear what is already inside you.

Accessing a Resourceful State

These questions ask you to remember a time when you felt confident, strong, or grounded. They help you explore how to bring that energy into the present.

Why this matters: You already carry the tools you need. These moments remind you of your strength and show you how to use it now.

Let these prompts be more than exercises. Let them be a practice. A ritual. A quiet space where you return to yourself again and again.

This is where your journey deepens.